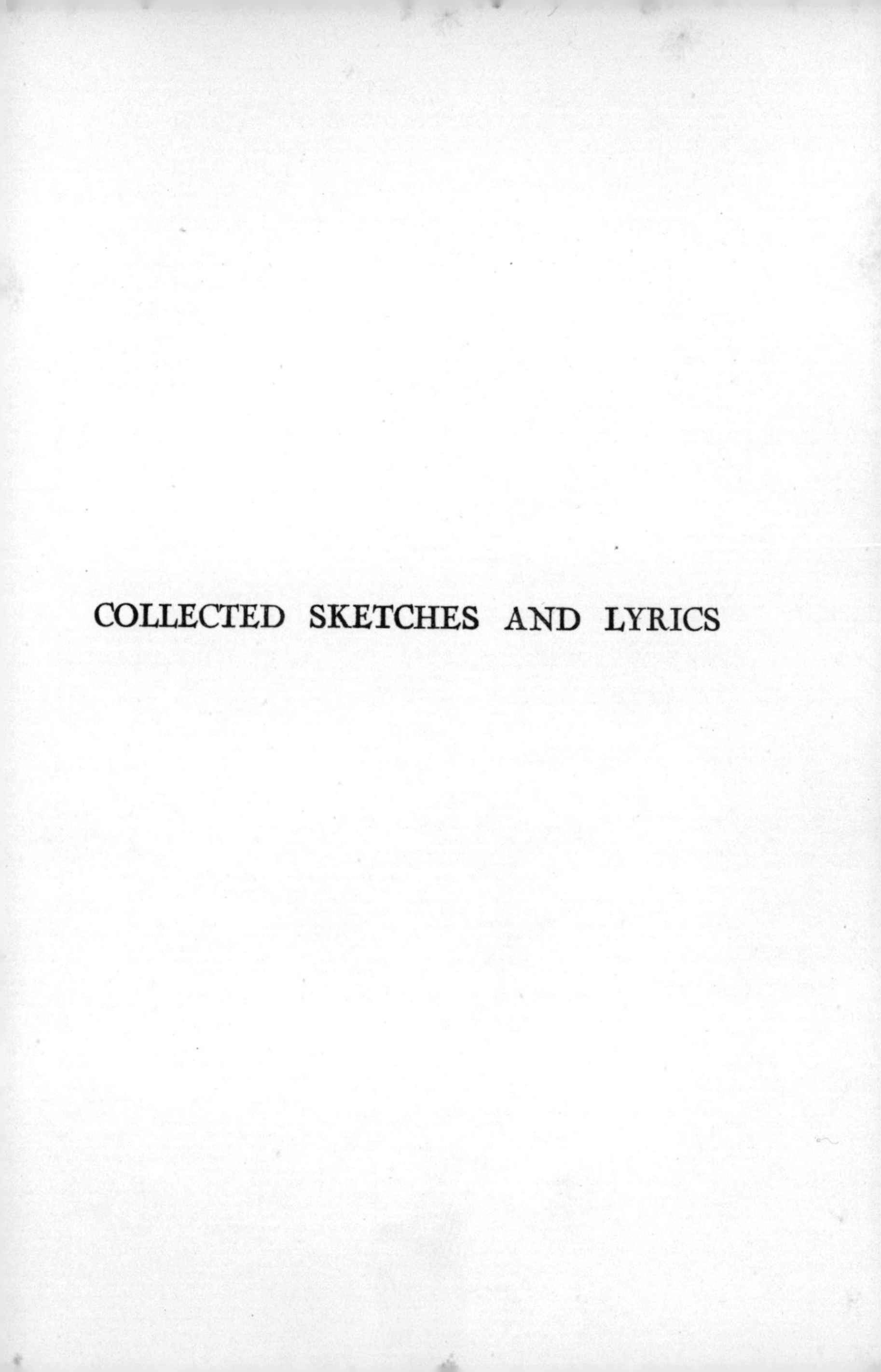

# COLLECTED SKETCHES AND LYRICS

# COLLECTED SKETCHES AND LYRICS

By

NOËL COWARD

SECOND IMPRESSION

HUTCHINSON & CO. (Publishers) LTD.
34-36 PATERNOSTER ROW, LONDON, E.C.4

Printed in Great Britain at
*The Mayflower Press, Plymouth.* William Brendon & Son, Ltd.

To ABEL

I DEDICATE THIS VOLUME TO YOU
IN MEMORY OF THE FRIENDSHIPS,
THE INTERESTS, THE GOOD ENTERTAINMENT
AND THE UNFAILING WELCOME I HAVE
FOUND AT THE IVY RESTAURANT
DURING ALL THESE YEARS

# EXPLANATORY PREFACE

The Sketches, Burlesques and Lyrics contained in this volume have mostly been selected from the following Revues: *London Calling* (1923), *On with the Dance* (1925), *This Year of Grace* (1928), *Cochran's* 1931 *Revue*, and *The Third Little Show* (New York, 1931). I have also included a few items which, for various reasons, have never been actually produced at all.

The art of Revue writing is acknowledged by those unfortunates who have had anything to do with it as being a very tricky and technical business. Everything has to be condensed to appalling brevity. The biggest laugh must be on the last line before the black out. No scene or number should play for more than a few minutes at most, and, above all, the Audience must never be kept waiting. The moment their last splendid laugh at the end of a sketch has subsided into a general chuckle, their attention must immediately be distracted by a line of vivacious chorus girls (preferably with bare legs) or a treble-jointed acrobatic dancer with no bones at all; in fact, anything arrestingly visual that will relax their strained minds and lull them into a gentle apathy while the next onslaught upon their risibilities is being prepared behind the scenes.

The lessons which have to be learned by aspiring Revue writers are many and bitter. The bitterest really being the eternal bugbear of "Running Order." Running Order is the sequence in which the various items in the show follow one another, and, however carefully the Author may have planned it originally, this sequence is generally completely changed by the time the show reaches dress rehearsal, and frequently drastically reorganised after the first night. For instance, the leading lady upon perceiving that the pretty blonde danseuse will undoubtedly make a tremendous success, resolutely refuses to follow immediately afterwards with her Powder-puff number with the girls, whereupon everything is changed round, and the low comedy lodging house scene is substituted in place of the Powder-puff number. Then, after a suitable interval, it is discovered that with this rearrangement it is impossible for the chorus to make their change from "The Jungle Scene" to the "Tower of London in 1586" because, according to the original lay-out, the six minutes lodging house scene came in between, whereas now they only have half a minute's reprise of the Theme song to enable them to get in and out of their wimples. At this point the Author is usually dragged, protesting miserably, into a cold office behind the dress circle and commanded to write then and there a brief but incredibly witty interlude to be played in front of black velvet curtains by no more than four minor members of the Cast (the Principals all being occupied with quick changes), without furniture, as there is no time to get it on and off, and finishing with such a gloriously funny climax that the Audience remain gaily hysterical for at least a minute and a half in pitch darkness.

Many of the small sketches in this book were created

in similar circumstances to those I have just described, and I must frankly admit that several of them look like it. Another problem which the writer has to face is the successful handling of Danger Spots. The principal danger spots in Revue are (1) The opening of the whole show, which must be original and extremely snappy. (2) The sketch immediately following it, which must so convulse the Audience that they are warmed up enough to overlook a few slightly weaker items. (3) The Finale of the first half. This should essentially be the high spot of the evening so that on the first night the bulk of the Audience and the critics can retire to the bars (if not already there) and, glowing with enthusiasm, drink themselves into an alcoholic stupor for the second half. The fourth danger spot is the strong low-comedy scene, which should be placed as near as possible to the second-half finale and should be strong, low, and very comic indeed.

If, upon reading the notices in the newspapers after the first night, it is found that different critics take exception to different scenes, you can safely predict a successful run. If all the critics unanimously take exception to one particular scene, it is advisable to move that scene to a more conspicuous place in the programme. If, on the other hand, no particular critic dislikes any particular scene and they all unite in praising the whole production, it either means that you have such a good show that they haven't the face to attack it, or such a bad show that they like it. In either case it will probably be a failure.

The various pieces collected in this book comprise the intermittent work of eight years, the first Revue with which I was ever associated being *London Calling*, which was produced by André Charlot at the Duke of York's Theatre in 1923. In this Revue I collaborated with Ronald Jeans on the book and Philip Braham on the music. Incidentally, I had the audacity to appear in it myself together with such assured Revue Artists as Maisie Gay, Tubby Edlin and Gertrude Lawrence. I appeared constantly throughout the show, singing and dancing and acting with unbridled vivacity, and enjoyed myself very much.

It was on account of the " Whittletot " sketch in this Revue that I unwittingly offended Osbert and Edith Sitwell. Some acrimonious letters were exchanged between Osbert Sitwell and myself, which we both enjoyed writing and reading, and the whole thing degenerated into a tiresome feud which continued convulsively for a few years, during which time we cut each other ostentatiously on every possible occasion and subjected many of our hostesses to delighted inconvenience.

A few years ago I met Osbert Sitwell in New York, and he was extremely nice about the whole affair and persuaded his sister by cable to forgive me, so the feud finally evaporated, for which I was exceedingly glad, as I should hate my whole-hearted admiration for the Sitwell family to be impaired by a personal matter of such small account.

In 1925 I worked for the first time for Charles B. Cochran and wrote *On with the Dance*, which was produced at the London Pavilion after a preliminary " try-out " in Manchester. The cast included Alice Delysia and Leonide Massine, who performed two ballets, also

Ernest Thesiger and Douglas Byng. It was a very heavy production, and our dress rehearsal in Manchester lasted from 10 a.m. on Monday until 1.30 p.m. on Tuesday without a break. As we took all that time to run through the show once, we arrived in the Theatre on the Tuesday night for the opening with considerable trepidation, but the performance went through without a hitch in two hours and three-quarters, which was, all things considered, nothing short of miraculous.

My next revue was also with Cochran at the Pavilion, *This Year of Grace* (1928), with a cast headed by Maisie Gay, Jessie Matthews, Sonnie Hale and Tilly Losch, and in America by Beatrice Lillie and myself.

A little while ago Charles B. Cochran wrote a brilliantly entertaining autobiography entitled *The Secrets of a Showman.* It is a glamorous book, closely packed with charmingly personal anecdotes, reminiscences, adventures and experiences, and contains probably fewer secrets than any autobiography ever published, because no showman worth twopence, let alone the greatest of them all, would be likely or even able to elucidate the methods by which he achieves his effects.

Whenever a liner stops at Port Said for coal, eager coloured gentlemen appear on board and perform for the passengers a series of incredible illusions. They talk incessantly all the time and say " Gilly Gilly " every other second. At the end of the entertainment they offer to sell the whole bag of tricks, with explicit directions, to any person who is fool enough to buy it. Now these gentlemen, within their limited scope, are merely coffee-coloured Cochrans. They produce live chickens from behind the ear with much the same finesse as Cochran produces lively comediennes from behind the " Madeleine," and they are perfectly willing to tell you all their secrets with the most amiable frankness, and in such a way that will successfully prevent you from comprehending one of them.

The secrets of Charles B. Cochran are even more elusive because they are the results of strange psychological abstractions which combine to make him a far more important figure than even his own book would have you believe. He is a sentimentalist with taste and a cynic with enthusiasm. He is an artist himself in his profound appreciation and understanding of artists. He has a kind heart, and I have never once seen him behave discourteously to any member of his companies. He is also as obstinate as a mule and resolutely refuses to be jostled in any direction, although I have known tactful coercion to work wonders. He has a useful and slightly uncontrolled passion for publicity. He has " Gilly Gillied " the Public unblushingly for years through the medium of the Press, and he has " Gilly Gillied " the Press for years on the security of his support from the Public. Taken all round, he is a very interesting character indeed, and I would rather work in association with him than any other manager in the world.

The selections in this book are from these three complete Revues I have mentioned, together with some oddments I have contributed from time to time to other shows.

As I have enlarged slightly on the anguish of Revue writing I tremble for those readers who take up this book optimistically prepared to conquer the art of Revue reading. Personally, I should imagine that for the layman a large portion of the following pages will be extremely bewildering if not actually unintelligible. I have purposely refrained from simplifying the stage directions, mainly because I think that would merely add to the general confusion. Regarding the various lyrics I have included I must implore the reader to remember that although they may not appear to scan on paper, they scan all right when fitted to their music; therefore in the case of those for which the music has not been published, I suggest that the reader makes up a little rhythm in his own head to fit the words. This occupation might conceivably pass many a long winter evening very unpleasantly.

I have left out most of the sentimental lyrics such as "A Room with a View," "The Dream is Over," etc. etc., because they really do look too silly in plain print. If some of the sketches appear to finish rather abruptly, please remember that that is the moment when the reader is expected to rock with laughter. A fuller effect might be obtained by reading the sketches aloud with one hand on the electric switch and on the last line plunging the room in darkness, thereby achieving as near as possible a "Black Out." I must say quite sincerely that I offer this book to the public with considerable misgivings, its only *raison d'être* being that it might afford mild amusement for amateur performances in the home (for any Public Performance a modest fee will be demanded on application to Curtis Brown, Ltd., 6 Henrietta Street, W.C.), or at least revive in the hearts of a few sentimentalists memories of one or two pleasant evenings spent in the Theatre during the last few years.

The dates affixed to the following items represent the year in which they were written rather than the year in which they were produced.

# CONTENTS

# COLLECTED SKETCHES & LYRICS

## MILD OATS

1922

(*When the curtain rises the stage is in darkness. There is the sound of voices. Enter* YOUNG MAN *followed by* YOUNG WOMAN. *He turns up lights, disclosing a comfortable little study with a sofa, arm-chairs, books, etc., and the remains of a fire in the grate.*)

HE. Won't you sit down?

SHE. Yes—thank you. (*She comes slowly down and sits on the sofa. She takes off her coat.*)

HE (*after a slight pause*). Do you know—the weather really is quite chilly.

SHE (*with an effort*). Isn't it? One can feel the tang of autumn in the air.

HE. Yes, one can.

(*Another pause.*)

SHE (*defiantly*). I *like* London in the autumn!

HE (*with equal defiance*). So do I!

SHE. It's so—so—melancholy.

HE. Yes—yes, melancholy—that's what it is.

SHE. What's the time?

HE (*glaring at his watch*). Half-past twelve.

SHE. It's late, isn't it?

HE. Very late.

SHE. What a pretty room.

HE. Yes, isn't it?—I mean—do you think so?

SHE. Oh yes—it's so—so cosy and home-like.

HE. I'm so glad.

SHE (*rising*). Books, too. Do you read much?

HE. Now and then. I mean—you know—sometimes.

SHE (*at shelves*). Nice books—specially that one.

HE. Which one?

SHE. Here—Strindberg.

HE. Oh, Strindberg—rather depressing fellow, isn't he?

SHE. Yes, but life—real life all the time—no false sentiment and—and—hypocrisy.

HE. Oh no, rather not—as a matter of fact I haven't read him much. This flat isn't really mine, you know—only lent to me.

SHE. Oh, I see. (*She sits down again.*)

HE. I haven't been here long.

SHE. It's very central.

HE. Yes—isn't it? (*Another pause.*) Would you like something to drink?

SHE (*quickly*). Oh no, thank you. (*Correcting herself.*) That is—perhaps—— (*With determination*) Yes, I would.

HE. I'm afraid there's only whiskey and soda. (*Crosses to table.*)

SHE (*blankly*). Whiskey and soda!

HE. Yes—is that all right?

SHE. Yes—that's all right.

HE. Say when.

SHE (*hurriedly*). Not much, you know—just a little —now—there—that's enough.

HE (*handing her a colourless drink*). It's very weak.

SHE (*shutting her eyes and handing it back*). Put some more whiskey in, then.

HE (*startled by her sudden vehemence*). Oh, all right— here you are.

SHE (*taking it*). Thank you—— (*She sniffs it.*) Oh dear!

HE. What is it?

SHE. Nothing——

(*She sips it and shudders. He doesn't notice.*)

HE (*sitting next to her on sofa*). Funny my meeting you like that.

SHE (*with a nervous laugh*). Yes—wasn't it?

HE. I could have sworn I'd seen you before somewhere.

SHE. I don't think so.

HE. Silly mistake to make. Look here, I——

SHE (*edging away*). What is it?

HE. Oh, nothing.

SHE (*after a pause*). I should like you to understand that——

HE. Yes?

SHE (*looking down*). Oh, nothing.

HE (*suddenly*). It's no use; I can't——

SHE. Can't what?

HE. Can't go on any longer. (*With vehemence*)

Look here, I don't care what you think of me—you're probably laughing up your sleeve all the time—but it doesn't matter—I mean—look here, will you go now?

SHE (*with her hand to her head*). You mean?—— Of dear! (*She faints on to his shoulder.*)

HE. Good God! (*He fans her.*) This is awful—awful! Wake up for heaven's sake—— Oh, this is terrible! (*He props her up with a cushion.*)

SHE (*opening her eyes*). Oh—what have I done?

HE. You fainted.

SHE (*bursting into tears*). Oh, this is awful—horrible! (*She leans on the edge of sofa and buries her head in her arms.*)

HE. I say, what's the matter? I didn't mean to be rude—honestly I didn't——

SHE (*sobbing*). I'm so ashamed—so dreadfully, dreadfully ashamed.

HE. Here, drink a little of this. (*He offers her her untasted drink.*)

SHE (*pushing it away*). Take it away, it makes me sick.

HE. All right. I say, I'm so sorry—do please stop crying.

SHE. Leave me alone—just for a minute, then I shall feel better. (*She sits up.*)

HE. I am a beast!

SHE. No you're not—that's just it—you're not, thank God. (*She rises.*) I must go at once.

HE. Where do you live?

SHE. Kensington.

HE. I'll see you home.

SHE. Oh no, please don't—it isn't necessary——

HE. I'll get you a taxi, then.

SHE. Very well—thank you.

HE. Wait here. (*He goes to door.*)

SHE. Stop.

HE (*startled*). What is it?

SHE. Please come and sit down—just for a moment. I want to tell you something——

HE. But——

SHE. Please—I really must—it may relieve this feeling of beastly degradation to tell you the truth——

HE. I wish you wouldn't look so unhappy.

SHE (*vehemently*). Unhappy! I'm desperately, bitterly ashamed—I've no words to express my utter contempt of myself——

HE. I don't understand.

SHE. I'm not what you thought I was at all.

HE (*embarrassed*). I didn't think you were after the first few minutes.

SHE. That's why you asked me to go?

HE. No, not exactly. I mean——

SHE. Oh, I am so grateful—you're a dear—I've been very, very fortunate—I—— (*She almost breaks down again.*)

HE. I say—please——

SHE (*pulling herself together*). All right—I won't cry any more—you must think I'm an abject fool—I am too—worse than that. Listen to me, I'm a perfectly ordinary girl—I live in Rutland Gate with my Aunt, I go to matinees and dances and walk in the Park and help get up Tableaux Vivants for charity——

HE. But—I——

SHE. Don't look so shocked—it makes it much harder to tell you everything—I read an awful lot—all the modern writers and the papers. I've over-educated myself in all the things I shouldn't have known about at all. I've been railing against the dullness of my life—a woman's life in general—I've read vehement feminist articles and pamphlets. I've worked myself up into a state of boiling indignation at the injustice of sex relationships—why shouldn't women have the same chances as men—lead the same lives as men—you know the sort of thing. I've been thinking myself a clever emancipated modernist—with a cool clear sense of values—and look at me—look at me—— (*She giggles hysterically.*) My Aunt went away to Bournemouth the day before yesterday for a week and I decided to make my experiment—to see life, real life, at close quarters—young men are allowed to go out and enjoy themselves when they're of age—why shouldn't young women have the same opportunities? Last night I went out to the theatre by myself and I started to walk home—feeling frightfully dashing—then it began to pour with rain, so I squashed into a bus and went straight to bed. To-night I was quite determined. I had dinner—by myself—at a place in Oxford Street, then I walked down into Piccadilly Circus—and down Haymarket and along the Strand, then back again to Leicester Square. I sat on a seat in the little garden place in the middle until a filthy drunk man came and sat down next to me—then I began walking again and looking at all the people—hundreds and hundreds of them—all pouring out of the theatres and crowding the pavements—it really was rather an exciting feeling—— You wouldn't understand it, I know, because you're a man and you haven't always been looked after and coddled all your life—you've been encouraged to be independent—but to me it was thrilling. I was all alone—absolutely my own mistress—then I suddenly realised how tired I was, so I went into Appendrodts and had a cup of chocolate. Two awful women were at the next table with a squirmy little man, and they started to have a row over his head—it was beastly—all the things they said—but very funny; in the end they were all turned out swearing like anything! Then I went out again and everything was different—all the crowds had disappeared and there was hardly any traffic except a few taxis going very fast. I walked all down Piccadilly—awfully quickly—because all the other women were sauntering so—I was just passing the Berkeley when an arc lamp in the middle of the road suddenly spluttered loudly—I nearly jumped out of my skin. Then I laughed at myself and began to walk more slowly—taking notice of things—the people's faces—it was strange—then—then—— Oh dear! (*She closes her eyes for a moment.*) Then a man smiled at me. I thought just for a second that I knew him, so I looked round and he was standing still. Then he began to stroll after me—my heart beat horribly and I strained every nerve to try to keep cool and think what to do—calmly—but I couldn't. I lost my head and ran up a side street like a rabbit—he must have laughed. Then I leant against some railings in Curzon Street and pulled myself together—I was a coward—a weak, silly coward, so then, more in order to punish myself for my lack of courage than anything else—I made up my mind to let a man—pick me up—— Oh, I know it's contemptible—don't look at me like that—but remember all this is the outcome of months—almost years—of modern literature—I wanted experience of life. Nothing could happen to me really—I'm quite capable of taking care of myself—I just wanted to see—then with the full flush of my determination still on me—I met you in Down Street. Oh dear, hasn't it been horrible! (*She sobs.*) Too utterly horrible for words——

HE. Look here, it hasn't really, you know—I won't breathe a word——

SHE. I know you won't—but—I don't feel as if I could ever shake off the shame of it——

HE. There hasn't been any shame——

SHE. I should like to go into a convent—straight away—this minute.

HE. You're taking it all much too seriously—it's funny rather—when you analyse it.

SHE. When I'm married and middle-aged I may look back upon it as being funny, but until then I shall blush down to my feet every time I think of it——

HE. I've never been out in London alone until this week—a friend of mine asked me up to stay here in this flat. Then he had to go away suddenly on business and so I was left on my own.

SHE. Is that true—really?

HE. Yes—that's why I asked you to go at first—I felt rotten.

SHE. Did you?

HE. Yes—absolutely. I thought you were laughing at me.

SHE. Laughing—— Good heavens!

HE. Yes—isn't it silly the way one is always so terrified of being laughed at?—it matters so little really.

SHE. Less than anything.

HE. All my friends talk such a lot about the gay times they have in Town—you know——

SHE. Yes.

HE. I thought to myself this is a wonderful opportunity—being alone—and everything——

SHE. Just like me.

HE. Yes—exactly——

SHE. How old are you?

HE. Twenty-one.

SHE. So am I.

HE. I'm most awfully sorry if I upset you and made you feel horrid.

SHE. You've been very kind and considerate. I don't know what I should have done if it had been anyone else.

HE. Neither do I.

SHE. I wish you'd empty that whiskey away—I do hate the smell of it.

HE. I'm not crazy about it. I say—shall we make some tea?

SHE. No, I must go now—really——

HE. It would be nice—are you sure?

SHE. Yes, quite—I must.

HE. All right. (*He goes to window.*) There's probably a cab in the rank. Why, it's pouring——

SHE. Oh! Is there a cab there?

HE (*looking out sideways against the glass*). No——Damn. I'm so sorry.

SHE. I'll soon find one.

HE. No—look here—do stay a little longer until the rain stops. We could have some tea after all——

SHE. But—but——

HE. We *are* friends—aren't we? (*He holds out his hand.*)

SHE. Yes—very well—just a little longer.

(*They shake hands.*)

HE. You'd better take off your coat again.

SHE. All right.

(HE *helps her off with it and puts it on chair.*)

HE. Now for some tea.

SHE. Where's the kettle?

HE. In the kitchen. I'll go and fill it and we can boil it in here—there's just enough fire. Will you get two cups out—they're in that cupboard, also some biscuits.

SHE. All right.

(HE *goes off.*)

(SHE *takes cups from cupboard and puts them on table, also a biscuit tin.*)

HE (*off*). How many spoonfuls in the pot?

SHE (*going to door*). Two, I should think—and a half a one.

HE. Righto.

(SHE *goes over and pokes up the fire a little.* HE *comes in with a small tray, upon which is a tea-pot and the kettle.*)

I haven't put much water in so it ought to boil quickly. (*He places it on the fire.*)

SHE. Now we must possess our souls in patience. (*She sits down on sofa.*)

He. We won't take any notice of it at all—we won't look round even if it sings.

She. Yes, I'm sure that's the only way.

He. What's your name?

She (*hesitatingly*). Oh——

He (*quickly*). I'm so sorry—I forgot—if you'd rather not tell me I shall quite understand—mine is Hugh Lombard.

She. Mine is Mary Jevon.

He. That's a pretty name.

She. I used to think it was much too phlegmatic and English—but still, if you think it's pretty——

He. Oh, rather—I like it all the better for being English.

She. So do I—in my heart—I've been hankering after something a little more exotic lately——

He. Further effects of modern literature on the young.

She. Now don't laugh at me——

He. Sorry.

She. You know what we are, don't you?

He. No, what?

She. We're the victims of civilisation.

He. Are we?

She. Yes we are—because we're really quite simple-minded and ordinary—deep down inside—but we've both been trying awfully hard to keep pace with the modern rate of living. If we went on much longer we'd kill all our real niceness——

He. I say, you know you are clever.

She (*suddenly*). Oh, don't—don't——

He. Don't what?

SHE. Don't pander to me—you'll undo all the good you've done!

HE. The *good* I've done—what *are* you talking about?

SHE. You've done me all the good in the world—you're thoroughly honest—and nice—and you're not really shocked at me and you like my name.

HE. I don't see where the good comes in?

SHE. You've saved me from myself—I know that sounds melodramatic—but it's true—absolutely.

HE. You've done the same for me—you made me feel awfully ashamed of myself—specially when you cried.

SHE. I am glad.

HE. So am I—why did you ask me not to pander to you?

SHE. Because I was being clever—and modern thoughtish——

HE. No you weren't—you were being sweet.

SHE. Don't be silly.

HE. But you were—awfully——

SHE (*vehemently*). Never again—never, never, never again.

HE. Never again what?

SHE. From this moment on I'm going to be myself—my real self—not my Chelsea edition——

HE. So am I—not my "young man about town" edition——

SHE. Splendid!

HE. I say—I've got an idea——

SHE. What——

HE. Look here—why shouldn't we——

SHE. The kettle's boiling.

HE. Oh—— (*He gets up.*) No it isn't.

SHE. I saw some steam coming out.

HE. Only very little—it fairly spouts when it's really ready——

SHE. What were you going to say?

HE. I won't say it yet—after all——

SHE. Why not?

HE. I'm afraid of spoiling things.

SHE. Oh!

(*They sit silent for a moment.*)

I wonder if it's stopped raining. (*She gets up and goes to window.*)

HE. Has it?

SHE. It's not so bad as it was—it's rather difficult to see here—one can only tell by the puddles.

HE (*joining her at window*). Aren't the pavements shining—like glass.

SHE. Yes, exactly—if you screw round the corner a bit you can just catch a glimpse of the Park. (*She flattens her face against the pane.*)

HE. Yes, it's jolly being so near——

SHE. What part of the country do you come from?

HE. Kent—the marshes.

SHE. No!

HE. Yes, why?

SHE. I know that well—between Rye and Folkestone——

HE. Yes—Ivychurch—my home's just near Ivychurch.

SHE. How lovely—it's beautiful on the marsh with all the dykes and space and the smell of the sea——

HE. I am glad you know it—and like it——

SHE. Look, the kettle really is boiling now.

HE. Come and hold the tea-pot.

(*They crouch together by the fireplace—and make the tea, then they put the pot on the tray.*)

Let's have it on the sofa—we can rest the tray on our knees.

SHE. All right. I'll sit down just—here—give it to me——

HE. All right—biscuits first.

(HE *places tin on the floor at their feet—then he hands her tray and sits down gingerly beside her.*)

SHE. Be careful.

HE. Isn't that cosy!

SHE. It isn't really drawn yet but it doesn't matter. (*She pours out.*)

HE. I don't think I've ever liked anybody so much—so quickly—before.

SHE. What nonsense!—— Sugar?

HE. Yes, please—two.

SHE. I've been pretending I like lemon in my tea for months—instead of milk.

HE. I know—so Russian!

SHE (*laughing*). Exactly——

HE. I really do want to say something—important—and you keep stopping me.

SHE. I know.

HE. Why——

SHE. For the same reason you said just now—it might spoil things——

HE. It wouldn't—I don't think——

SHE. Don't let's risk it—yet.

HE (*gloomily*). All right——

(*They drink in silence for a moment.*)

SHE. What do you do?

HE. How do you mean?

SHE. Work.

HE. I'm going to be a soldier.

SHE. Oh——

HE. The worst of it is—it will probably mean India——

SHE. Oh, that kind of soldier.

HE. Yes—life on verandahs with punkahs waving and clinking ices in tumblers and beautiful catty women in sequin dresses——

SHE. And spotless white breeches and polo ponies and sudden native risings and thrilling escapes—lovely!

HE. Do you think you'd like it?

SHE. Yes—anyhow at first—it sounds so—so different.

HE. I'm glad you don't hate the idea——

SHE. What's the time?

HE (*putting down his cup*). Early—look. (*He shows her his watch.*)

SHE (*putting down her cup with a bang*). I must go now—at once—really I must.

HE. Oh——

SHE. Even if it's coming down in torrents—— (*She goes to window.*)

HE. I wish you'd stay—a little longer.

SHE. No—it would be silly to linger on—I feel frightfully tired and I'm sure you are too—we should only get sleepy and bored. The rain's quite stopped—and there's actually a cab there——

HE. Damn it!

SHE. Now then!

HE. I wanted to walk with you until we found one.

SHE. You can walk with me all the way downstairs.

HE. All right.

SHE. Help me with my coat.

HE. Here.

(HE *helps her on with her coat—then he takes her hand.*)

Thank you ever so much—it's been lovely.

SHE. Yes, it has——

HE. Let me say it—now.

SHE. What?

HE. Will you marry me?

SHE. Don't be silly.

HE. I'm not silly. I mean it.

SHE. We don't know one another.

HE. Yes, we do—frightfully well.

SHE. No—it's too soon.

HE. I'm beginning to love you terribly——

SHE. No you don't—not really—you can't——

HE. Why not?

SHE. I don't know.

HE. Time doesn't make the least difference—you *know* it doesn't.

SHE. Perhaps—perhaps it doesn't——

HE. Could you ever care for me—do you think?

SHE. I don't know.
HE. Will you try?
SHE (*nods*). Don't—else I shall cry again.
HE. You are a dear!

(HE *takes her in his arms and kisses her.*)

SHE (*tremulously*). Now my hat's crooked——

(*They go out together, his arm protectively round her.*)

CURTAIN

## "HE NEVER DID THAT TO ME"

1924

I

I HAVE been a Movie fan
Since the cinemas first began;
My young brother's a camera-man,
   And when I start
Meeting heroes of romance,
I shall firmly take my chance,
Though I find the hero's charming,
I prefer the more alarming
   Man who plays the villain's part.
The things he does to nice young girls,
   Aren't easy to forget;
He never minces matters,
   When he traps them in his net.

*Refrain* 1

He never did that to me;
He never did that to me;
Though I must admit,
He wasn't a bit
Like what I'd supposed he'd be;
The way that he uses
Ingenues is

Really a sight to see;
He binds them across his saddle tight,
Regardless of all their shrieks of fright,
And carries them upside down all night,
He never did that to me.

*Refrain 2*

He never did that to me;
He never did that to me;
Though I must admit,
He wasn't a bit
Like what I'd supposed he'd be;
I once saw him save a Christian slave,
And gallantly set her free.
She knelt at his feet with downcast head,
"God will reward you, sir," she said.
He gave her a look—and struck her dead;
He never did that to me.

2

Though my disappointment's great,
I shall never procrastinate,
I've determined to watch and wait,
And then you'll see;
He'll revert to type, perhaps,
Have a violent moral lapse,
When the moment's quite propitious,
He'll do something really vicious,
Think how lovely that will be.

His reputation's terrible,
  Which comforts me a lot ;
If any girl is seen with him,
  She's branded on the spot.

*Refrain* 1

He never did that to me ;
He never did that to me ;
Though I must admit,
He wasn't a bit
Like what I'd supposed he'd be ;
We went in his car,
But not too far,
Some mutual friends to see ;
The car gave a lurch and then a skid,
We didn't turn over—God forbid !
Whatever you may have *thought* he did——
He never did that to me !

*Refrain* 2

He never did that to me ;
He never did that to me ;
Though I must admit,
He wasn't a bit
Like what I'd supposed he'd be.
I once saw him fish the Sisters Gish
From out of the stormy sea ;
He locked them in his refined Rolls Royce,
And said in a most determined voice,
" It's death or dishonour—take your choice ! "
He never did that to me !

# DEVON

## 1920

I

You men may quaff your frothing ale,
  From tankards, mugs and pots,
But Devonshire's the only place
  To find for-get-me-knots.
    The earth is red,
    The beer is red,
  The girls are redder still,
The sun looks down with a roguish eye,
  So up your glasses fill,
Fill up, fill up, fill up, fill up, fill up.

*Refrain*

Oh ! some may go to Clacton,
  And some may care for Bude,
You may laugh ho ! ho ! at Felixstowe,
  Though as a resort it's rather rude.
Oh ! some may go to Bognor,
  Or Ashton-under-Lyne,
But Francis Drake cried Todaloodaloo,
  In Devon by the Brine.

2

But when life's sky is overcast
  And death is in the vale,
Though we may go to rest at last,
  Thank God we've got our Ale.
For Devon men are red throughout
  In April, May and June,
So let your sturdy voices shout,
  For Drake and Lorna Doon,
Hey Doon, Fie Doon, Fie Doon, Fie Doon,
    Fie Doon.

*Refrain*

Oh ! Wigan men are hearty
  And Bolton men are bold,
There's something coy in a Blackpool boy,
  And the Bedford lads have hearts of gold,
But the chaps that live on Dartmoor
  Are breezy, bright and gay,
  Singing a tra la la
  With a hey ho ha
  And a whack fol do
  And a nin noni no
  And a down derry down, sing hey,
  Down derry down, sing hey,
Ha ha, ha ha, ha ha, ha ha, ha ha, ha ha, ha ha,
  ha ha.

# CARRIE

1922

*Verse* 1

CARRIE as a baby was a darling little pet,
And everybody loved her, from the Vicar to the Vet,
Her manners when at school were most ingenuous and quaint,
She had the reputation of a little plaster saint.

*Refrain* 1

Carrie was a careful girl,
Such a very careful girl,
Nobody imagined from the day that she was weaned,
That underneath her sweetness was the temper of a fiend.
Carrie was a careful girl,
Quite a little cultured pearl,
The teachers all adored her and the pupils did the same,
At every sort of girlish sport she quickly made a name,
And nobody suspected that she played a double game,
Carrie was a careful girl.

*Refrain 2*

Carrie was a careful girl,
Such a very careful girl,
She stole out on the landing while the others were at prayers,
And rubbed a lot of grease upon the dormitory stairs.
Carrie was a careful girl,
In her little cot she'd curl,
The teacher fell down half the flight and landed on her head,
And naturally to Carrie not a single word was said
'Cos they found a pat of butter in her little sister's bed,
Carrie was a careful girl.

*Verse 2*

Carrie had a father with a rather mottled past,
And evils of heredity are bound to show at last,
But Carrie always realised the danger from the start,
So she stole dear father's diary and learnt it off by heart.

*Refrain 3*

Carrie was a careful girl,
Such a very careful girl,
When papa departed to the angels meek and mild,
He left a lot of souvenirs and maxims to his child.
Carrie was a careful girl,
And when in the social whirl,

Though she wasn't tempted by the usual forms of vice,
She said she thought that games of chance were really awfully nice.
But still she never played a game without her father's dice,
Carrie was a careful girl.

*Refrain* 4

Carrie was a careful girl,
Such a very careful girl,
So far and no further she was quite prepared to go,
But still she took precautions 'cos of course you never know.
Carrie was a careful girl,
Once she met a noble Earl,
He thought that Carrie lived alone and so she let him think,
She asked him to her flat one night to have a little drink,
But she had her Auntie Jesse underneath the kitchen sink,
Carrie was a careful girl.

(*Repeat end of Refrain*)

Carrie was a careful girl,
Once she met a noble Earl,
She gave him the impression that she didn't know the ropes,
But when he got impassioned and began to raise her hopes,
She bought herself the latest book by Dr. Marie Stopes,
Carrie was a careful girl.

# WEATHERWISE

## 1923

### A COMEDY IN TWO SCENES

### CHARACTERS

| | |
|---|---|
| LADY WARPLE | |
| MONICA } CYNTHIA } VIOLET } | *Her daughters.* |
| THE REV. HAROLD BASSET | *Monica's husband.* |
| REGGIE WHISTLER | |
| BUTLER | |
| DR. TWICKENHAM | *A Psycho-Analyst.* |

*The action takes place in the Library of Warple Manor in the County of Leicestershire.*

*One week elapses between* SCENES *I and II.*

### SCENE I

*When curtain rises, it is late afternoon, after tea.* LADY WARPLE *is knitting by the fire—she is a dignified and slightly austere-looking old lady.* REGGIE WHISTLER, CYNTHIA *and* VIOLET *are seated about smoking.*

CYNTHIA. And, my dear—they went up and touched him and the body was still warm!

VIOLET. What a perfectly horrible story—it gives me the creeps—ugh! (*She shudders.*)

REGGIE. You don't seriously believe in it though, do you?

CYNTHIA. Of course I do.

VIOLET. Don't you scoff, Reggie, there are more things in heaven and earth than are dreamt of in man's something or other.

REGGIE. I'm not scoffing, but I must say I think this pyschic business has been rather overdone lately.

VIOLET. It's sometimes very useful, Gloria Frimpton found out all about her first husband through a fortune-teller.

REGGIE. Only because he happened to be living with the fortune-teller at the time.

CYNTHIA. Not living *quite*—just visiting occasionally, but still it only shows——

LADY W. I fear, Violet dear, that you have not placed before Reggie's doubting mind a really convincing example of the marvels of Psychic Research. You have both witnessed, in my presence, the most amazing demonstrations—I cannot imagine why you have not quoted them to prove your point. Take for instance our wonderful conversation with your dear Auntie Clara only last Thursday. We actually heard her voice, did we not?

CYNTHIA. Yes, Reggie, we did honestly.

REGGIE. I don't see how; if she's nothing but a spirit I doubt if she even has a larynx.

VIOLET. I don't believe one speaks with one's larynx, anyhow.

REGGIE. Auntie Clara *always* did, it was one of her greatest charms.

LADY W. Even though you are an old friend of the family, Reggie, it is hardly nice of you to be facetious on such a subject.

REGGIE. But are you quite certain that you weren't all thinking of her so hard that the sound of her voice was a sort of subconscious suggestion?

LADY W. Quite certain. But if you're determined not to believe in a thing, of course you won't. Nothing can ever be proved without Faith.

CYNTHIA. You're being very tiresome, Reggie.

REGGIE. Not at all, I want to be convinced frightfully badly.

VIOLET. Nonsense, you laugh at everything.

LADY W. I read a dreadful story in the *Psychic Herald* the other day, about a woman who refused to believe—and one evening when they were doing a little table turning after dinner—she went off into a trance.

REGGIE. I frequently go off into a trance after dinner.

CYNTHIA. Don't interrupt, Reggie.

LADY W. I repeat, she went off into a trance, and when she came to, she was found to be possessed by an evil spirit.

VIOLET. Mother—you never told us that.

CYNTHIA. What did it make her do?

LADY W. I couldn't possibly repeat it out loud—bend forward.

(CYNTHIA *leans forward and* LADY WARPLE *whispers in her ear.*)

CYNTHIA. How appalling!

VIOLET. You must tell me, Cynthia.

(VIOLET *bends forward and* CYNTHIA *whispers in her ear.*)

I suppose they had to dismiss the butler in sheer self-defence.

LADY W. Yes, but with a handsome compensation.

VIOLET. Naturally.

LADY W. To my mind there's something absolutely terrifying in the thought of being possessed—unconsciously possessed—by an alien spirit.

CYNTHIA. Didn't she know anything about it?

LADY W. Not until afterwards when they told her, then she went mad and imagined she was Charlotte Corday—— It was all very awkward as they had a Cabinet Minister staying in the house at the time and she kept trying to get into his bathroom.

VIOLET. Poor dear, how awful!

LADY W. Eventually she had to be sent away, that sort of thing is so likely to be misconstrued—especially in Leicestershire.

REGGIE. That theory does account for a lot though. Sophie Flotch was behaving in a most peculiar way in the Ritz last week, I think her possessive spirit must be an emu, or something equally unbecoming.

CYNTHIA. Oh mother, do let's do the Ouija board for a little while, I feel wonderfully eerie inside—we might get thrilling results.

REGGIE. What is a Ouija board?

VIOLET. My dear, don't you know? They're marvellous things.

CYNTHIA. Like Planchette you must have seen them.

REGGIE. How many can do it at the same time?

VIOLET. Only two, but one has to sit by the side and write down the answers.

LADY W. It would be absurd to attempt it with Reggie in the room.

REGGIE. No it won't—I'm absolutely serious—do get it, Violet.

VIOLET. All right, pull the blinds down—it's here I think.

(*She goes over to desk and searches.* REGGIE *proceeds to pull the blinds down.*)

REGGIE. Surely if it's pitch dark we shan't be able to see anything at all.

CYNTHIA. It's not going to be pitch dark, there'll be firelight—very ghostly and effective—draw up the chairs closer, Reggie.

VIOLET. Here it is—anyone got a pencil?

REGGIE. Yes.

(*They assemble round a small table by the fire—* CYNTHIA *takes* REGGIE'S *pencil and balances a Bridge marker on her knee.*)

CYNTHIA. You and Violet had better begin, mother —it always starts more quickly for you than anyone else.

LADY W. I don't feel well enough to-day, dear—I'll just sit here and listen.

VIOLET. Come along then, Reggie, rest your hands quite lightly on it, and for heaven's sake don't sneer, because it's frightfully unlucky. Can you see to write, Cynthia?

CYNTHIA. Yes, but I'm not going to write all the time, I want to work the thing too.

REGGIE. We'll take it in turns.

LADY W. If it starts to say rude things like it did to Fanny Belton, you'd better stop immediately.

VIOLET. Don't press so hard.

REGGIE. I'm not.

VIOLET. What shall we ask it?

CYNTHIA. You'd better find out if it's there first.

VIOLET. All right. (*Whispering mysteriously*) Is anyone there?

(*There is a slight pause, then the board begins to move.*)

REGGIE (*looking carefully*). It says "No."

CYNTHIA. That's absurd.

VIOLET. You pushed it, Reggie.

REGGIE. I did not push it.

CYNTHIA. Ask it again.

VIOLET. You, this time, Reggie.

REGGIE (*obediently*). Is anyone there?

(*The board moves again.*)

CYNTHIA (*looking*). No.

REGGIE. This is ridiculous—there must be someone there to say "No."

VIOLET (*with superiority*). It often behaves like this at first—one must have patience.

REGGIE. Never mind if it's there or not, let's ask it a question.

VIOLET (*to the board*). Are you an Elemental?

(*The board moves.*)

CYNTHIA (*looking*). No!

REGGIE. The thing's stuck.

VIOLET (*perseveringly*). Who are you?

(*The board moves.*)

CYNTHIA (*spelling out*). QUEEN VICTORIA.

REGGIE. My hat!

VIOLET. Shut up, Reggie—— (*To board*) Have you a message for us?

(*The board moves.*)

You pushed it then, Reggie, I saw you.

REGGIE. I did *not* push it.

CYNTHIA. If you go on quarrelling over it, you can't expect it to answer.

REGGIE. She was probably pushing it herself and trying to put the blame on me.

VIOLET (*hotly*). Reggie, how *can* you tell such lies.

CYNTHIA. Oh, for goodness sake ask it what its message is.

VIOLET (*to board*). Have you got a message for us?

(*The board moves.*)

CYNTHIA (*looking*). Yes.

REGGIE (*to board*). What is it?

(*The board moves.*)

CYNTHIA (*spelling out*). WE ARE NOT AMUSED. It's Queen Victoria all right.

REGGIE. That's because we quarrelled—I suppose

we'd better apologise—— (*To board*) We're awfully sorry.

VIOLET (*to board*). Have you any other message for us?

(*The board moves.*)

CYNTHIA (*looking*). Yes.

REGGIE (*intensely*). What is it?

(*The board moves.*)

CYNTHIA (*spelling out*). BOW—BOW.

VIOLET. Reggie was pushing—I felt him all the time.

REGGIE. I wasn't—I swear I wasn't—Queen Victoria really meant Bow-wow.

VIOLET. Look out—it's moving again——

(*The board moves quickly.*)

CYNTHIA (*spelling out*). WHAT—DREADFUL—WEATHER——WHAT—DREADFUL—WEATHER——OH—DEAR—OH—DEAR—BOW—BOW.

(*Enter* MONICA. *Lady Warple's eldest daughter, with her husband, the Rev.* HAROLD BASSET. *They turn up lights.*)

MONICA. What are you all doing in the dark?—We've been for a splendid tramp, right through the village and round.

VIOLET. Oh, Monica—you've ruined our séance.

REV. BASSET (*confidingly to* CYNTHIA). Yes, right through the village and round, we went—most delightful—such a holiday for me after my parish work in Shadwell.

MONICA. Not that absurd thing again, Violet—

really you are ridiculous—it would have done you all more good to be out in the fresh air—we've had a ripping walk.

REGGIE. Right through the village and round?

MONICA. Yes.

REGGIE. I thought so.

MONICA (*quietly to* CYNTHIA). You know perfectly well I asked you not to encourage mother in all this spiritualistic nonsense, she takes it seriously and it's very bad for her.

REV. BASSET. If it had been intended that we should communicate with the other world, it would have been made easy for us.

REGGIE. Nothing could be easier than sitting here with a Ouija and talking to Queen Victoria.

CYNTHIA. Look at mother, what's the matter with her?

VIOLET. She's asleep.

MONICA. That will mean a headache all the evening. (*She goes over to* LADY WARPLE.) Wake up, mother.

(LADY WARPLE *remains quite still.*)

Wake up, mother!

VIOLET. Something's happened—she's not asleep—look at her eyes, they're open. (*She rushes to* LADY WARPLE *and shakes her.*) Mother—mother—wake up!

MONICA. Feel her heart, quick.

(VIOLET *does so.*)

VIOLET. It's beating all right.

MONICA. Fetch some brandy, Harold, at once.

(*The* REV. HAROLD *departs hurriedly into the dining-room.*)

CYNTHIA. Brandy's no use—don't you see—she's in a trance!

MONICA. A trance?

CYNTHIA. Yes, and it's our fault for conjuring up evil spirits. Oh, what are we to do, what are we to do?

REGGIE (*with a certain amount of relish*). Burn feathers under her nose—that always brings people to——

(*He seizes a large brocade cushion and having set light to it, brandishes it about over* LADY WARPLE.)

MONICA. Reggie, that was one of the best brocade cushions.

REGGIE (*waving it about*). Of course, brocade smoke is much more pungent than the ordinary kind.

(*Re-enter the* REV. HAROLD *with brandy and a glass.*)

REV. BASSET (*excitedly*). Here you are—here's the brandy.

MONICA (*taking complete command of the situation*). Give it to me.

(MONICA *tries to make* LADY WARPLE *swallow some brandy.*)

CYNTHIA (*suddenly*). My God!

MONICA. What is it?

VIOLET. What's the matter?

CYNTHIA. Violet—Reggie—don't you remember—a trance—the woman who thought she was Charlotte Corday——

VIOLET. You mean mother might be—— Oh dear, oh dear!

MONICA. What on earth are you talking about?

CYNTHIA (*breathlessly*). There was a woman who went off into a trance and they told her afterwards and she thought she was Charlotte Corday, and she tried to get into the bathroom with a Cabinet Minister and——

REGGIE. Well, we needn't worry about that yet—the nearest Cabinet Minister is twelve miles away at Warborough.

MONICA. Are you all stark staring mad—what do you mean?

VIOLET. I'll explain. You see, when people go off into trances there's always the fear that when they come to they may be possessed by some alien spirit. Mother read about a woman in the *Psychic Herald* who—— (*She whispers in* MONICA'S *ear.*)

MONICA. Great heavens! But how could she do it in the time?

REV. BASSET. I'm sure that a dutiful Christian woman like your mother could never be possessed by anything unpleasant—the disembodied spirit of some noble heroine perhaps—working for the good of mankind——

REGGIE. Well, let's all hope it doesn't turn out to be Joan of Arc; think how embarrassing it would be if she persistently rode to hounds in shining armour.

MONICA. Look—look—she's coming to——

CYNTHIA. Don't tell her she's been in a trance *whatever* happens.

LADY W. (*drowsily*). What a dreadful smell of burning.

MONICA. Here, mother dear—sip some of this.

LADY W. How can you, Monica, you know perfectly well I hate brandy; what are you all looking so frightened for?

MONICA. Well, mother—you see—you've just fainted and we——

LADY W. (*crossly*). Fainted! What nonsense—I've never fainted in my life—good gracious! One of my best cushions—who did this? (*She holds it up furiously.*)

REGGIE. I did—I think it saved your life.

LADY W. Have you all taken leave of your senses? Where's my dinner?—I want my dinner.

CYNTHIA. It isn't quite time for it yet, mother dear.

REGGIE (*softly to* VIOLET). It's all right, she's only been possessed by a hearty appetite.

LADY W. I want my dinner.

VIOLET. We're all going up to dress in a moment.

LADY W. I must go out soon.

CYNTHIA. Go out? Why—where?

LADY W. Don't all jump at me like that every time I say anything; surely there's nothing extraordinary in wanting to go out?

REV. BASSET. It would have been quite understandable this afternoon—but now it's simply pouring—really you never know where you are with the English climate——

LADY W. (*growls softly*). Grrrrr! Grrr!

REV. BASSET. I beg your pardon.

MONICA. What did you say, mother?

LADY W. (*ferociously*). Grrrr—Grrrr—Grrrrrrr!!!

CYNTHIA. Good heavens—what's she doing?

(LADY WARPLE *suddenly takes a flying leap from her chair and growling and barking furiously proceeds to career round the room on all fours—everybody shrieks.* MONICA *makes an effort to stop her but is severely bitten for her pains.* CYNTHIA *and* VIOLET *jump on to the sofa and* REGGIE *takes refuge on the club fender.* MONICA, *weeping with pain and fright, clambers with her husband on to the writing-desk.* LADY WARPLE *with yaps and growls of delight seizes the remains of the cushion in her teeth and worries it round the room, occasionally sneezing playfully and tossing the feathers in the air.*)

REGGIE (*from the fender—soothingly*). Down, sir; down, sir, down!

(LADY WARPLE *crouches on the rug more or less quietly and continues to tear the cushion with less ferocity but great concentration.*)

CYNTHIA (*from the sofa*). It's a dog—a dog—mother's been possessed by a dog.

REGGIE. Yes—and I *think* it must be a bull terrier.

MONICA (*furiously*). Surely this is no time to discuss the breed.

REGGIE. It's always better to be accurate—then we shall know what to say to the authorities.

VIOLET (*in tears*). Authorities—authorities—you mean——? Oh, this is horrible—horrible.

REGGIE. It's not the slightest use getting hysterical—we must keep quite calm and think things out—she'll probably get dangerous again when she's finished that cushion; perhaps we'd better ring for a bone or something——

MONICA. Don't you dare—we must get her up to bed without the servants knowing. (*Ingratiatingly to* LADY WARPLE.) Here then—here then—good dog—good ole doggie——

(LADY WARPLE *snarls and shows her teeth.* REGGIE *jumps down fearlessly from the fender, pats* LADY WARPLE'S *head, and then pats the seat of her arm-chair insinuatingly. With a little snort she ambles across and jumps up into it, then with all the family breathlessly watching she straightens out her legs and settles herself into an ordinary human position with her eyes closed.*)

REGGIE (*in a hoarse whisper to everybody*). For heaven's sake don't mention the weather—that's what does the trick.

VIOLET. That's what the Ouija meant when it said, "What weather—bow-wow!"

REGGIE. Exactly.

CYNTHIA. Oh, this is too frightful for words—poor, poor mother.

VIOLET. I wish it had been Charlotte Corday now, or even Lucrezia Borgia—they were quiet!

REGGIE. Shhhh!!!

(LADY WARPLE *slowly opens her eyes and looks round absently.*)

LADY W. Has anyone seen my knitting?

QUICK CURTAIN.

## SCENE II

*One week later.*

(*When curtain rises,* MONICA, CYNTHIA, VIOLET, *the* REV. HAROLD, *and* REGGIE WHISTLER *are all standing near the door back centre—in rather strained, listening attitudes.)*

REGGIE. Unless she breaks out and does something violent he'll think we've been lying.

VIOLET. Perhaps he hasn't mentioned the weather yet.

MONICA. Didn't you tell him to?

VIOLET. No, somehow I felt that it sounded so silly.

MONICA. My dear Violet, it's sheer stupidity to try to hide anything from a doctor, specially a Psycho-Analyst—he must know every symptom if he is to cure her.

CYNTHIA. So far he's done nothing but question her about her childhood—I can't think why.

REV. BASSET. I believe it is in order to discover the roots of her complexities—I've heard the subject discussed—very interesting indeed.

REGGIE. He seemed awfully upset when she answered the hoop question.

CYNTHIA. I didn't hear that—what did she say?

REGGIE. Well, apparently she was a year later than the average child in bowling her first hoop—which made her correspondingly backward with her doll's perambulator.

VIOLET. Did he attach any awful significance to that?

REGGIE. He shook his head gravely and asked her if she'd ever broken a slate at school.

MONICA. Yes, I heard him—I'm sure it's all rubbish.

REGGIE. Not at all—I believe in it all implicitly—of course it's bound to take time—going through every small incident of her childhood—these Psycho-Analysts are marvellous—they always find something in the end.

CYNTHIA. She was possessed last Tuesday by that beastly dog, and nothing will convince me to the contrary, whatever he says, it was all our fault—she'll be wanting to go out sooner or later, and think what will happen if anyone comes up and says, " What a fine day it is " or something—she'll fly at them and bite them.

REV. BASSET. Have you tried prayer?

CYNTHIA. Yes, and without the slightest effect.

VIOLET. What are we to do if he can't cure her?

REGGIE. Well, it depends if she gets better or worse —I should refrain from chaining her up in the yard for as long as possible.

MONICA. Shhh! Here comes the doctor!

(*Enter* DOCTOR EVERARD TWICKENHAM, *the eminent Psycho-Analyst—he has spectacles and a rather supercilious expression.*)

MONICA. Well?

DOCTOR. There is no cause for alarm.

REV. BASSET. God be praised.

DOCTOR (*breathing on his glasses and polishing them*). For a long while I delved unsuccessfully in the slightly complicated psychology of her childhood—then suddenly I hit—quite by accident—upon the root of the evil.

VIOLET. What was it?

DOCTOR (*complacently*). Your mother's nurse—I gather from her descriptions rather a gaunt woman—upon her fourth birthday, snatched from her hand a small woolly dog on a stand—recently given her by her

Auntie Jessie—and in a moment of anger struck her sharply on the head with it. This thoughtless act in due course formed a complex in the child's mind, the active results of which you have all witnessed.

REGGIE. They were certainly active.

MONICA. Are you sure that that was the cause, Doctor Twickenham?

DOCTOR. Quite convinced of it, my dear Mrs. Basset.

VIOLET. I have a sort of confession to make, Doctor.

DOCTOR. Well, well, well, what is it?

VIOLET. I told you the story of the Ouija board and Queen Victoria and everything, but I omitted one fact——

DOCTOR. Yes?

VIOLET. You haven't seen mother during one of her attacks, have you?

DOCTOR. Unfortunately not—but it is of no vital consequence.

VIOLET. Well, I never told you the actual cause of her outbreaks.

DOCTOR (*testily*). Surely I mentioned that I've discovered the cause for myself.

VIOLET. But you haven't—I mean—you never discussed the weather with her at all, did you?

DOCTOR. No, but all this is beside the point.

VIOLET. It *isn't* beside the point—because the weather is what makes her bark.

DOCTOR (*smiling pityingly*). My dear Miss Warple—please forgive me—but really—it's too absurd.

REGGIE. It's the truth, Doctor.

DOCTOR (*severely*). Perhaps you will allow me to know

best, young man. I have made a thorough examination and I'm perfectly satisfied that—providing you carry out my instructions—your charming hostess will be her normal self by this evening. It is all extremely simple, I have worked it out psychologically. The only thing required to cure her completely is a sudden shock, and what is more, a shock possessing some relation to her present mental condition.

MONICA. How do you mean, Doctor?

DOCTOR (*consulting his watch*). It is now nearly four-thirty—in a few moments tea will be brought in, will it not?

CYNTHIA. Yes.

DOCTOR. Excellent—that is by far the best time.

REGGIE. The best time for what?

DOCTOR. Control your impatience, young man, and attend carefully. Miss Warple, your mother—being unaware of the peculiar malady from which she is suffering—will come down to tea as usual—I too will be present and we will all talk and laugh in an ordinary manner. Suddenly I will blow my nose loudly like this—(*he does so*)—then, having claimed your undivided attention, I shall say "Bow-wow" softly. At this signal you will instantly proceed to emulate the manners and habits of dogs, making as much noise as you can. The unexpected sound of everybody barking and growling will undoubtedly restore the old lady's mind to its normal condition, and the canine complex will—by sheer force of concentrated suggestion—be completely exorcised.

CYNTHIA. Is that the only way?

DOCTOR. Absolutely.

MONICA. I suppose it wouldn't do if we got Rover in and hid him under mother's chair?

VIOLET. Rover's bark is beautifully piercing.

DOCTOR. That would not be sufficient—concerted effort is essential.

MONICA (*unhappily*). Very well—you'd better ring for tea at once, Reggie, and we'll get it over.

VIOLET. I'll go and fetch mother.

(*She goes out.*)
(REGGIE *rings bell.*)

MONICA. Forgive our apparent lack of enthusiasm over your suggestion, Doctor—but we have all been in an exceedingly nervy state during the last week—what with trying to keep everybody off the subject of the weather, and trying to hide the truth from the servants—it's all been very, very uncomfortable.

CYNTHIA. Only this morning mother had an outbreak all by herself and disappeared—I think she must have been reading the forecast in the *Daily Mail*.

DOCTOR. Where did she go to?

CYNTHIA. We discovered her on one of the upper landings tearing the cook's bedroom slippers to pieces.

MONICA. That sort of thing is so dreadfully difficult to explain; of course we told cook it was Rover, but she looked awfully suspicious. She'll probably give notice soon.

REV. BASSET. And on Sunday evening we found out that—— (*He whispers to the* DOCTOR.)

DOCTOR. What on earth did you do?

REV. BASSET. We said it was Rover!

(*Enter* BUTLER *with tea-things, which he arranges round fire, and exits.*)

REGGIE. You won't say Bow-wow until I've had at least three hot cakes, will you, Doctor?

MONICA. Don't be so selfish, Reggie—you know we want to cure mother as soon as possible.

CYNTHIA. How long are we to go on being dogs?

DOCTOR. Until I shout Bow-wow a second time, then you must all run out of the room, and leave me alone with your mother.

MONICA. I do hope the Dermotts won't call—we should never hear the last of it.

(*Enter* LADY WARPLE *leaning on* VIOLET'S *arm.*)

LADY W. Ah, Doctor, I'm so glad you're staying—so far everyone refuses to tell me what is the matter with me—perhaps tea will make you a little less reticent on the subject; I know it can't be anything really serious because I feel so extraordinary well.

MONICA. It's nothing to worry about in the least, mother dear—come and sit down.

(LADY WARPLE *is installed in her usual chair*—MONICA *proceeds to pour out the tea, while* REGGIE *hands round the cakes.*)

LADY W. Hand me my knitting, will you, Violet dear—it's on the window seat.

VIOLET (*gives her knitting*). Here it is—you've nearly finished it.

LADY W. It's been a terrible nuisance—I get so tired of these depressing sales of work.

DOCTOR. Have you always been a parish worker?

LADY W. Now he's going to ask me some more embarrassing questions—I never know what to answer.

REGGIE (*with tea-cup*). Here's your tea, Doctor.

DOCTOR. Thank you so much.

LADY W. As if I could possibly remember Burglar Bill.

CYNTHIA. Burglar Bill?

LADY W. Yes, I recited it at my school concert when I was six.

DOCTOR. Never mind, we jogged your memory a bit, didn't we?

LADY W. Only to the extent of my saying "Wat's oo doing Mr. Wobber." I'm sure that couldn't have conveyed anything to you.

DOCTOR (*jovially*). Ah well—I'll explain my methods at more length another time.

CYNTHIA (*softly, in answer to a whispered question from* VIOLET). No, I shall just whine—that's all.

LADY W. What did you say, Cynthia dear?

CYNTHIA (*airily*). Nothing, mother—nothing particular——

REGGIE (*to the* DOCTOR *in a hoarse voice*). You can go ahead now I've eaten four.

LADY W. I wish you'd all stop whispering to one another—it's exceedingly irritating.

REGGIE. I'm sorry.

LADY W. When I was eight and a half I can remember quite distinctly being sharply slapped for whispering.

DOCTOR. Ah!

LADY W. (*reminiscently*). I was in the schoolroom at the time—Elizabeth Spoopin had come to tea with me—fancy—her daughter had twins only last week, how time flies——

(*The* DOCTOR *with a look at everyone blows his nose loudly.*)

LADY W. (*jumping*). My dear man, what a start you gave me.

DOCTOR (*austerely*). Bow-wow !

LADY W. (*astonished*). I *beg* your pardon.

(*With a howl,* CYNTHIA *jumps on to the sofa, where she begins to scratch excitedly, whining loudly all the time.* MONICA *and* THE REV. HAROLD *leap on to the hearthrug on all fours—yapping hideously, where they proceed to worry mythical bones.* REGGIE *with a loud bark chases* VIOLET *round the room on all fours, then he catches the hanging edge of the table-cloth in his teeth and pulls everything to the ground—then he and* VIOLET *nozzle the cakes along the carpet with their noses. The concerted noise is deafening. The* DOCTOR *stands in the background with a watch in his hand.* LADY WARPLE *looks startled for a moment and then bursts out laughing.*)

(*Weakly.*) Absurd creatures—how ridiculous you are !

(*She proceeds with her knitting, laughing fondly. The family make renewed efforts to rouse her but with no success ; at last the* DOCTOR *steps forward.*)

DOCTOR (*loudly*). Bow-wow !—— (*Nobody hears him at first, so he has to bellow at the top of his voice.*) BOW-WOW ! !

(*The family all make a dive for the door—still yapping and barking and growling—leaving the* DOCTOR *and* LADY WARPLE *alone.*)

LADY W. Have you ever known anything so ludicrous —really I'm surprised at Harold—the children have always loved practical jokes and booby traps, but he never seemed to have enough spirit for that sort of thing until to-day.

DOCTOR. Lady Warple—I want you—if you don't mind—to look straight into my eyes.

LADY W. (*putting down her knitting*). Must I?

DOCTOR. If you please.

LADY W. (*staring into his eyes*). Is that right?

DOCTOR. Thank you—yes—I am now perfectly satisfied you are now completely and absolutely cured.

LADY W. I'm so glad, and I'm sure you've been awfully clever, but would you be so kind as to tell me what has been the matter with me?

DOCTOR. Just a slight nerve complex, that's all. You must go on being comparatively quiet and take as much fresh air as possible without over-tiring yourself—luckily the cold snap is over and the weather has become delightfully mild again——

(*Before he has time to defend himself,* LADY WARPLE *with a fearful growl makes a spring at his throat—in a moment she gets him on to the ground and worries him like a rat—snarling ferociously. He gives one loud cry which brings all the others rushing into the room.* MONICA *with a shriek pulls* LADY WARPLE *off him, and* REGGIE *bends down and feels his heart. Then he gets up.*)

REGGIE (*shaking his head sadly*). He's quite quite dead! Now we shall have to destroy Rover!

CURTAIN

## CUSTOMS HOUSE, DOVER

1923

### CHARACTERS

JOE BUSH *Customs Official*
ENGLISHMAN
" GET AWAY GRACE "
DETECTIVE
LULU HIGGINS

(*When curtain rises the noise is deafening—the chorus in various travelling dresses are clustered round the low counter, trying to get the baggage examined quickly, and talking and shouting. Above the din can occasionally be heard the* OFFICIAL'S *voice saying :* " *Now then, now then—anything to declare?* " *etc. After a moment the noise subsides a little and a few spaces are left on the counter. A young* ENGLISHMAN *strolls languidly in and planks his suitcase down in front of the* OFFICIAL.)

OFFICIAL. Anything to declare—wines—spirits—cigars ?

YOUNG MAN. Damn all.

OFFICIAL. What d'you mean by that ?

YOUNG MAN. Damn all.

OFFICIAL. Damn all what?

YOUNG MAN. Damn all to declare.

OFFICIAL. Look 'ere, don't you try to be funny with me, see!

YOUNG MAN. Why not?

OFFICIAL (*blustering*). Never mind why not! Just open up—come on now. (*Delving in bag.*) What's this?

YOUNG MAN. Hair wash—what did you think it was, pink champagne?

OFFICIAL. You think you're very clever, don't you?

YOUNG MAN (*languidly*). Not particularly, but I think you're extremely stupid.

OFFICIAL (*leaning forward*). Do you know I'm old enough to be your father?

YOUNG MAN. Yes—and almost silly enough.

(*He goes off.*)

(*The* OFFICIAL *scratches his head for a moment. Enter a beautifully dressed* GIRL *with a small dressing-case—she places it in front of the* OFFICIAL.)

GIRL. Will you wait just a minute while I find the key?

OFFICIAL. Anything to declare—wines, spirits, cigars?

GIRL. Well, as a matter of fact there is the teeniest bottle of scent.

OFFICIAL. 'Ow big?

GIRL (*leaning towards him*). Not very big—but I'll show you when I've found the key.

OFFICIAL. It's all right, Miss, there ain't no 'urry.

GIRL. Oh, but there is—it's so irritating to me to keep you waiting when you're probably so tired—oh, where can it be?

OFFICIAL. Well, I dunno—what about your 'andbag?

GIRL (*quickly*). Oh no, it wouldn't be in there—I remember now—I tied it on to a little bit of ribbon round my neck. (*She puts her hand up and produces a small piece of blue ribbon—then she gives a little cry.*) Oh!

OFFICIAL. What's up?

GIRL. It's gone.

OFFICIAL. Gone where?

GIRL. Dropped off.

OFFICIAL. P'raps it's slipped down the back.

GIRL. I wonder if you'd look for me. (*She leans towards him backwards across the counter.*)

OFFICIAL. I'll do my best.

GIRL. Put your hand there. (*She places his hand in the small of her back—he slips his arms round her waist—she breaks away with a little cry.*) Officer—that was very naughty of you!

OFFICIAL. I'm sorry, miss—I forgot meself, I——

GIRL (*bursting into tears*). Oh, this is dreadful, dreadful, what am I to do?

OFFICIAL. Oh, look 'ere, don't cry, Miss—it don't matter.

GIRL. Oh, but it does—it does—I know you think I'm smuggling through all sorts of awful things—and how can I prove to you that I'm not, without my key——? (*Her voice trails off into sobs.*)

OFFICIAL. 'Ere, miss—— (*He chalks her bag.*) We won't say anything about that bottle of scent—this time, see.

GIRL (*sniffing*). Oh, Officer, I wouldn't get you into trouble for anything in the world.

OFFICIAL. That'll be all right, Miss——

GIRL. You're very, very kind—I suppose you couldn't lend me a hanky? Mine's in the bag. (*She sobs again.*)

OFFICIAL. Now then, now then, 'ere you are—— (*He hands her an enormous handkerchief.*)

GIRL. Thank you. (*She wipes her eyes.*) Thank you very much. (*She leans her head back—he gives a quick glance round, then kisses her.*) (*Coyly*) Oh, Officer! (*She blows a kiss to him, and taking her dressing-case, runs off.*)

(*A* MAN *in a bowler hat and overcoat, obviously a plain clothes detective, comes in hurriedly—he goes up to the* OFFICIAL.)

DETECTIVE. Here—I want a word with you.

OFFICIAL. All right, what's up?

(*He gets over the counter and they both come down stage.*)

DETECTIVE. "Get Away Grace" left Paris last night; she's been traced as far as Calais.

OFFICIAL. "Get Away Grace"?

DETECTIVE. She's one of the most notorious dope traders in the world—she smuggles the stuff through from Toulon and Marseilles.

OFFICIAL (*apprehensively*). What's she like?

DETECTIVE. She's quite young really, but she generally disguises herself as an older woman—she'll probably wait until the night boat, there are fewer people about.

Just keep your eyes open, see—search every bag thoroughly—I'll be within call if you whistle——

OFFICIAL. But—but——

DETECTIVE (*in warning tones*). And if I were you I should be a little more spry—you've let a lot of stuff through lately—we've watched you—you're slack—stupid—lazy—see?

OFFICIAL. Oh yes, I see.

DETECTIVE. And if you don't manage to nab someone or something pretty soon you'll lose your job, see?

OFFICIAL. Oh yes, I see.

DETECTIVE (*going off*). So mark my words, and try to be a little more intelligent, see?

(*Exit.*)

OFFICIAL. Oh, go to 'ell.

(*He goes dismally back to the counter, a loud engine whistle is heard, there comes an answering shriek from the boat. Enter* LULU HIGGINS. *She is a flashy, overdressed woman of about forty, her hair is tousled and her hat over one eye, she has long buttoned boots all unbuttoned—she has obviously been exceedingly seasick. A porter follows her wheeling a professional hamper on a trolley, it has* HIGGINS *painted on it in black letters.*)

LULU (*shrieking*). 'Old it back! 'Old it back! Oh, young man, 'old it back.

OFFICIAL (*stopping her*). Steady on now—'old what back?

LULU. The train, of course. Oh, God, I've been so ill—lying on that boat in a state of coma.

OFFICIAL. Well, you've reached your full stop now all right. (*He clutches her arm.*)

LULU. Let me go—let me go!

(*There is another engine whistle off.*)

OFFICIAL. Anything to declare?

LULU. Nothing, I swear I 'aven't.—Oh, let me go!

OFFICIAL. What's in that 'amper?

LULU. Only me props——

OFFICIAL. Props. I don't think—open it up——

LULU. Let me go, you great hulking brute.

(*Another loud whistle, then a sound of a train starting.*)

OFFICIAL. Too late.

LULU (*bursting into tears*). There now, it's gone—and it's all your fault—— Oh, if only the Baron were here——

OFFICIAL. Never mind the Baron—open up.

LULU. It's only me props and me night things.

OFFICIAL. Why isn't it registered, it ain't 'and baggage?

LULU. 'Cos I wouldn't trust anything I valued on these railways alone—lot of nasty lying thieves and rogues.

OFFICIAL. Rogues, are we—rogues!

LULU. Yes, rogues and vagabonds—and if only the Baron were here he'd let you 'ave it!

OFFICIAL. Where's your key?

LULU (*giving it to him*). 'Ere. Fat lot you'll find.

OFFICIAL. I know what I'll find all right.

LULU. Well then, all I can say is that you ought to be ashamed of yourself.

(OFFICIAL *flings open the lid of the basket, various articles fall out.*)

OFFICIAL. 'Ere we go.

LULU (*enraged*). Oh, it's scandalous—that's what it is, to think of all the sacred objects of a woman's toilet being mauled about by a great uncouth brute.

OFFICIAL. 'Ere, 'old on, 'old on, less of that.

LULU. Oh, I wish I could say in English what the Baron thinks in French.

OFFICIAL (*holding up a paper package*). What's this?

LULU (*trying to snatch it*). Give it to me!

OFFICIAL (*pulling it about*). Ah! I've caught yer this time.

LULU. Leave it alone.

(*They both pull the paper off and a bundle of underclothes falls to the ground. The* OFFICIAL *picks them up but* LULU *grapples with him.*)

Give them to me, I'll teach you to mess about with my free-and-easies! (*She snatches them from him.*)

OFFICIAL. It isn't any treat to me.

LULU. Oh yes it is, you're revelling in it, that's what you're doing—revelling in it—I can see it in your eye.

(*He continues to rout about among her things.*)

It's no use raking about with that, you won't find any hidden treasure in my hot-water bottle.

(*He holds up a bottle.*)

OFFICIAL. What's this?

LULU (*airily*). Just some very expensive French stuff to make your face lovely.

OFFICIAL (*putting it back*). You'd better keep that.

LULU (*bitterly*). Oh, if only the Baron were here.

OFFICIAL. Now look here, I know you've got that dope somewhere—you'd much better own up.

LULU. Who d'you think you're talking to, young man?

OFFICIAL. "Get Away Grace!"

LULU. "Get Away Grace" me foot! My name's Lulu Higgins.

OFFICIAL. Lulu Higgins!

LULU (*gathering up some of the scattered clothing and putting them back in the hamper*). Yes, what's the matter with it?

OFFICIAL (*dazed*). Lulu Higgins?

LULU. Yes—why—what's the matter——?

OFFICIAL. Lulu—it's Joe—don't you remember—Joe Bush?

LULU. Well, I'm——

OFFICIAL. You—of all——

LULU. Good heavens!

OFFICIAL. After all these years.

LULU. Old Joe Bush.

(*They fall into one another's arms.*)

OFFICIAL. But, Lulu, you're a big star now—it's wonderful!

LULU. And look at you—all got up in gold braid and everything.

OFFICIAL. Been playing over there?

LULU. Yes—Folies Bergeres they call it—and the things they wanted me to do—really those French! I know we're all made more or less alike, but there's no need to flaunt it.

OFFICIAL. What sort of stuff d'you do?

LULU. I'm a "Dieseuse," dear.

OFFICIAL. What's that?

LULU. God knows, but it's very lucrative.

(*They both close the hamper and sit side by side on the lid.*)

OFFICIAL. Who's that Baron you've been talking about so much, your husband?

LULU (*giggling*). Oh, don't be such a fool!

OFFICIAL (*sadly*). Oh, Lulu, have you broken that vow we made in the old days?

LULU. What vow?

OFFICIAL. We both swore we'd never do anything we'd be ashamed of.

LULU. Well, *I* don't—it's the Baron.

OFFICIAL. What's he like?

LULU. Not bad.

OFFICIAL. You know, you've changed, Lulu—you're more worldly than you used to be.

LULU. Well, you'd be worldly if you'd been Queen in the Ballet of Love for eighteen weeks.

OFFICIAL. What were you in before that?

LULU. Doing a turn of me own on the halls—very trying work—and so cosmopolitan—d'you know at one place I topped the bill with a troupe of performing animals?

OFFICIAL. Very lowering to your prestige, that sort of thing.

LULU. I don't know about me prestige, dear, but the way those monkeys used to go on in between the shows!

OFFICIAL. Do you remember when you were bitten by that bull terrier coming out of the theatre at Huddersfield?

LULU. How we laughed!

OFFICIAL. And d'you remember what you found in your bed at Oldham?

LULU. That wasn't at Oldham!

OFFICIAL. And when you upset cocoa down your dressy blouse!

LULU (*sighing*). It seems quite like old times sitting on this old prop basket.

OFFICIAL. 'Ow many years is it since we first met—it was at Leeds, wasn't it?

LULU. Yes, Wilson Barret opened on the Monday at the Grand with *The Sign of the Cross* and we were in *Hey Diddle Diddle* at the Empire.

DUET: "TOURING DAYS"

OFFICIAL. Lulu.
LULU. Joe.
OFFICIAL. It's many years ago
Since we took the British drama by the throat.
LULU. How time flies!
OFFICIAL. You've increased in weight and size.
LULU. I feel thinner since I left the beastly boat.

OFFICIAL. I can remember
Late in November,
Opening in Ashton-under-Lyne.
LULU. Your suit was sweet,
With a patch in the seat
For the sake of Auld Lang Syne.
BOTH. Touring days, Touring days,
What ages it seems to be,
OFFICIAL. Since the landlady at Norwich
Served a mouse up in the porridge,
And a beetle in the morning tea.
BOTH. Touring days, Touring days,
Far back into the past we gaze,
OFFICIAL. They battered in your luggage once at Miller's Dale,
LULU. I had to wrap my washing in the *Daily Mail*,
OFFICIAL. The platform looked exactly like a Jumble Sale,
BOTH. Those wonderful Touring Days!

BOTH. Touring days, Touring days,
LULU. I frequently call to mind
What you said to Mrs. Bluett
When you broke her silver cruet
And she made you leave your watch behind.
BOTH. Touring days, alluring days,
Far back into the past we gaze,
OFFICIAL. The landlady was always drunk at Aberdeen,

She used to keep her money in the soup tureen,

LULU. One night you swallowed half a crown and turned pea-green,

BOTH. Those wonderful touring days.

BOTH. Touring days, Touring days,
What glorious lives we led,

OFFICIAL. Was it *Caste* or *Julius Cæsar*
When you blew up with the geyser,
And I dragged you from the bath half dead?

BOTH. Touring days, Touring days,
Far back into the past we gaze,

OFFICIAL. Do you remember playing in *The Shulamite?*
Your understudy greased your rubber heels for spite,

LULU. I fell and broke me contract on the Friday night,

BOTH. Those wonderful Touring Days.

## PARISIAN PIERROT

1923

*Verse*

Fantasy in olden days,
In varying and different ways,
  Was very much in vogue.
Columbine and Pantaloon,
A wistful Pierrot 'neath the moon,
  And Harlequin a rogue.
Nowadays Parisians of leisure
  Wake the echo of an old refrain,
Each some ragged effigy will treasure
For his pleasure
Till the shadows of their story
  Live again.

*Refrain*

Parisian Pierrot,
Society's hero,
The Lord of a day,
The Rue de la Paix
Is under your sway.
The world may flatter,
But what does that matter?

They'll never shatter
Your gloom profound.
Parisian Pierrot,
Your spirit's at zero,
Divinely forlorn,
With exquisite scorn
From sunset to dawn
The limbo is calling,
Your star will be falling,
As soon as the clock goes round.

---

## "THERE'S LIFE IN THE OLD GIRL YET"

1923

*The scene is a garden, the* CHORUS, *male and female, are standing about in various stages of self-conscious ease.*

1ST CHORUS GIRL. Isn't this a delightful garden, Lady Nora?

2ND GIRL (*in stilted tones*). Yes, indeed it is, Lady Angela.

3RD GIRL. They say dear Kitty 'tends each flower with her own fair hands.

1ST CHORUS BOY. How topping!

2ND BOY (*loudly*). Here comes Lady Kitty.

(*The orchestra strikes up the introductory bars of her song and* LADY KITTY *enters laughing girlishly, and carrying a basket of roses in one hand and a very fluffy parasol in the other. She is rather fat, with metallic golden hair, her dress is extremely "bitty," with rose-buds and small bows wherever they are humanly possible. As she reaches the centre of the stage the music stops and the chorus cluster round her all talking at once. As she speaks they form a large semicircle round her.*)

LADY KITTY (*vivaciously*). Isn't it all just too beautiful for words!

1ST BOY (*self-conscious and extremely Cockney*). Oh! Lady Kitty, you are fairer than all the blooms in your lovely garden.

LADY KITTY (*laughing musically*). Ah! flatterer, see, I have a rose for every one of you so that none shall be jealous.

2ND BOY. Oh! Lady Kitty, you are a tantalising little rogue.

LADY KITTY. I know, I know, but that's just my way.

(*Cue for Song:*)

*Verse 1*

LADY KITTY.

I'm a naughty little lady,
Full of winsome girlish tricks,
Though I'm rather past my heyday
I began with Seymour Hicks,
With the Chorus Boys behind me
I'm a sight you can't forget,
Though the years have rather lined me
I am still a firm Soubrette.

CHORUS BOYS.

Tell us why, tell us which,
Tell us what, tell us how,
Tell us when, tell us soon,
Tell us *now*.

*Refrain* I

LADY KITTY. They call me Kitty.
CHORUS. Why?
LADY KITTY. Because I'm pretty.
CHORUS. Ah!
LADY KITTY. And because I have a dainty curl.
CHORUS. Naughty girl!
LADY KITTY.
Then preserve me and woo me and ask me to dine,
But I'm always in bed by a quarter past nine,
I'm awfully sporty,
And I'll be forty.
CHORUS. When?
LADY KITTY. On October the twenty-third.
CHORUS (*derisively*). What a bird!
LADY KITTY.
Though there may be one or two notes that I can't quite get,
CHORUS. Well——
LADY KITTY. There's life in the old girl yet.

*Verse* 2

LADY KITTY.
I'm as playful as a kitten,
Love has seldom passed me by,
I have more than once been bitten,
But I'm hardly ever shy—

Though if Winter came—my style would—
  Be a little undermined,
Still, the spring of second childhood—
  Can't be very far behind.

CHORUS BOYS.

Pretty soon, pretty near,
Pretty quaint, pretty queer,
  Pretty Poll, pretty pet,
Pretty dear.

*Refrain 2*

LADY KITTY. They call me Flossie.
CHORUS. Why?
LADY KITTY. Because I'm mossy.
CHORUS (*firmly*). Yes.
LADY KITTY. And because I always go the pace.
CHORUS (*rudely*). Shut yer face!
LADY KITTY (*coyly*).
I show traces of laces and silk underneath,
I'm as young as my tongue, but much older than
    my teeth,
  My goodness gracious!
CHORUS. Well?
LADY KITTY. I'm so vivacious!
CHORUS. Hell!
LADY KITTY. Always ready for a kiss or two.
CHORUS. Fancy you!

LADY KITTY.

Though at one time people always called me
"Gladstone's Pet,"
Still there's life in the old girl yet.

(*The dance should be extremely complicated, involving general movements with a parasol, kicking over the handle occasionally successfully—generally not. Then sitting on each of the* CHORUS BOYS' *knees with a quick turn between each. Finally, after many gyrations and a lot of brightness being carried off very uncomfortably shoulder high.*)

## THE SWISS FAMILY WHITTLEBOT

1923

(IN A SHORT EXPOSITION OF MODERN ART)

(MISS HERNIA WHITTLEBOT *should be effectively and charmingly dressed in undraped dyed sacking, a cross between blue and green, with a necklet of uncut amber beads in unconventional shapes. She must wear a gold band rather high up on her forehead from which hang a little clump of Bacchanalian fruit below each ear. Her face is white and weary, with a long chin and nose, and bags under the eyes. Her brothers* GOB *and* SAGO WHITTLEBOT *are dressed with self-conscious non-chalance in unusual clothes.* GOB *wears cycling breeches and a bottle-green velvet coat with a big floppy bow, cloth-topped boots and a tweed shooting hat.* SAGO *is faultlessly dressed in a slightly Victorian morning suit. His shirt and boots are not quite right and his silk hat is upside down by his side. Their musical instruments are rather queer in shape.*

(MISS HERNIA WHITTLEBOT *speaks.*)

"It is difficult for me to explain to you in words that which I have to say regarding Life, and Art, and Rhythm. Words are inadequate at the best of times. To me life is essentially a curve, and Art an oblong within that curve. Rhythm is fundamental in everything. My brothers and I have been brought up on Rhythm as other children are brought up on Glaxo. Always we have tried to create Sound and Reality and Colour. My brothers, on their various instruments (and they have many), and myself, with all the strength and courage I can summon up, will endeavour to prove to you the inevitable Truth in Rhythmic Colour Poetry. People have jeered at us, often when walking in the street they have thrown fruit and vegetables at us, but it is all colour and humour. We see humour in everything, especially the primitive.

My first Poem is an early Peruvian Love Song."

(*Accompanied in fitful gusts by* GOB *and* SAGO *she recites.*)

Beloved, it is Dawn, I rise
To smell the roses sweet,
Emphatic are my hips and thighs,
Phlegmatic are my feet.
Ten thousand roses have I got
Within a garden small,
God give me strength to sniff the lot,
Oh let me sniff them all.

Beloved, it is Dawn, I rise
To smell the roses sweet,
Emphatic are my hips and thighs
Phlegmatic are my feet.

(*The next poem strikes an exultantly gay note—the colours are vivid and ruthless because they are Life.*)

Rain, Rain, Pebbles and pain,
Trickle and truckle and do it again,
Houpla, Houpla, Dickery Dee,
Trolderol trolderol, fancy me.

(*Musical interlude.*)

Fancy me !

I will now recite my tone poem " Passion " to which special music has been set by my brother Gob on the Cophutican.

Passion's dregs are the salt of life
Spirits trodden beneath the heel of
Ingratitude.
Drains and Sewers support the quest
Of eternal indulgence.
Thank God for the Coldstream Guards.

I will now give you a very long and intensely primitive poem entitled " The Lower Classes." I have endeavoured to portray the bottomless hostility of the Labour Party towards themselves and everybody else—I wrote most of the first part in a Lighthouse.

(*At this moment sounds become audible from the Prompt Corner. The* STAGE MANAGER *is making signs to them that their time is up.*)

War and life and the Albert Bridge,
Fade into the mists of Salacious obscurity
Street hawkers cry apathetically
Mothers and children rolling and slapping
Wet on the grass—I wonder why.
Guts and Dahlias and billiard balls
Swirling along with spurious velocity
Ending what and where and when
In the hearts of little birds
But never Tom Tits.
Freedom from all this shrieking vortex
Chimneys and tramcars and the blackened branches
Of superfluous antagonism
Oxford and Cambridge count for naught
Life is ephemeral before the majesty
Of Local Apophlegmatism
Melody semi-spheroidal
In all its innate rotundity
Rhubarb for purposes unknown, etc. etc.

(*The* STAGE MANAGER *having despaired of making her hear, has signed to the Orchestra to strike up the next number. Unmoved by this* MISS WHITTLEBOT *produces a megaphone—at last in desperation the* STAGE MANAGER *begins to set the next scene and the* WHITTLEBOT FAMILY *are eventually pushed off the stage still playing and reciting*)

# "SORRY YOU'VE BEEN TROUBLED"

1923

CHARACTERS:

POPPY BAKER
MAID

(*When curtain rises* POPPY *is discovered asleep in bed. A breakfast tray is on a small table on her left, and a telephone on her right. Sunlight is streaming across the bed—the telephone rings violently.* POPPY *slowly wakes up.*)

POPPY (*sleepily*). Oh damn! (*She takes off receiver and speaks with a pronounced Cockney accent.*) 'Allo! 'Allo! Who is it, please? Mr. Pringle—— No, sir—I'm afraid Miss Baker isn't awake yet—— Oh no, sir—I daren't, sir—she'd sack me on the spot, sir—yes, sir—— Good-bye, sir. (*She slams down receiver crossly.*) Old fool, waking me up!

(*She takes the breakfast tray from side table and rests it on her knees. She proceeds to pour out coffee, she sips some of it and then begins to eat a little toast. The telephone rings again. She takes off receiver and speaks with her mouth full.*)

'Allo, 'allo—who is it speaking? (*Abruptly changing her voice.*) Maggie darling, is it you?—— Yes, I thought it was old Potty Pringle—twice this morning, dear, really it is the limit, he ought to be at home dandling his grandchildren—— Oh yes, dear, orchids as usual —very mouldy looking with rude speckles all over them, but still they *are* expensive—what! *No!*—— You haven't got your Decree Nasty or whatever it is?—— Darling, I'm frightfully glad—— Well, if dragging you to the Beggar's Opera fourteen times isn't cruelty, I don't know what is—— You'll have to be awfully careful now for six months, won't you?—— Well, you'd better leave Claridge's and go to the Regent Palace, you'll be safer there—— Do you mean to say the Judge actually said that to you in Court?—— What a dreadful old man—but they're all the same, dear, no respect for one's finer feelings—— Fanny? Oh no, it was quite different with her, she won her case on points like a boxer—— No, nothing was ever proved because though she started for Brighton four times with the worst possible intentions, she never got further than Haywards Heath—— Well, dear, I really am most awfully glad—— I suppose they'll give you the custody of the Daimler—— What? Oh no, darling, no such luck, I heard from him yesterday—he won't let me divorce him—— Beast!—— It isn't as if we were fond of one another, I haven't set eyes on him for five years—— Yes, he's with Freda Halifax now, she got him away from Vera—I believe she's driving him mad —serve him right—what I think of husbands!—— O no, Bobbie's different—besides, he isn't yet, I don't suppose he ever will be. (*She sniffs.*) You know, I love him terribly—— Don't go on giggling—— All right, Ciro's at one o'clock.

(*She puts receiver on and resumes her breakfast. Her expression is rather pensive and she occasionally sniffs pathetically. The telephone rings again, she answers it.*)

Hallo—— Hallo—— Yes, who is it?—— What? —— I can't hear. What? Oh the line's buzzing—— Yes, yes, speaking—— Police Station! Why—what's happened?—— Yes—— Last night—— Oh, my God!—this is terrible—— Yes, at twelve o'clock—— I say—listen—— Oh, they've cut me off!

(*She puts the receiver on again and sits in stricken silence for a moment. She bites her lip and dabs her eyes with her handkerchief—then a thought strikes her—she grabs the telephone.*)

Hallo—— Exchange—get me Mayfair 7160 at once—— Yes—— Claridges?—— Put me through to Mrs Fanshaw, please—— Oh, quick, quick, it's urgent—— Hallo—— Maggie—— Maggie, is that you?—— Oh, my dear, listen, the most awful thing—the police have just rung me up—— Jim jumped over Waterloo Bridge last night—— No, darling, I don't know what time—— Yes, I knew you'd be sympathetic—— That's a little callous of you, dear; remember he *was* my husband after all—— I'm wretched—utterly wretched—— Yes, naturally they communicated with me first, how were they to know we hadn't seen each other for years?—— Oh, it's awful—awful! Yes, Ciro's one o'clock (*She hangs up receiver for a moment, then bangs lever violently.*) Hallo—— Hallo—— Kensington 8712—yes, quickly. Hallo, is that you, Flossie? Poppy speaking—— My dear, Jim's dead! (*She sniffs.*) Thank you, darling, I knew you'd be a comfort—— No, dear, he jumped off Waterloo Bridge—— Yes, the one next to Charing Cross—— No, no, no, *that's* Blackfriars. Don't be so silly, Flossie, you know perfectly well Westminster comes first, then Charing Cross—the one with trains on it, *then* Waterloo—— Oh, how *can* you—you do say the most dreadful things, you'll only make me break down again in a minute—I'm having such a struggle—such a bitter, bitter struggle—— (*She sobs.*) Anyhow, I'm quite successful enough without that kind of advertisement—— Look here, lunch with Maggie and me at Ciro's one o'clock—— All right—*thank you,* darling. (*She hangs up receiver again. Then after a moment's pause she calls up.*) Hallo, hallo, Regent 2047, please—yes—I want to speak to Miss Hancox, please —— Yes, it's important—— Hallo, is that you, Violet? Poppy speaking. You know when you told my cards the other day you told me something dreadful was going to happen? Well, it has!—— Oh, no, darling, not *that,* anyhow I haven't seen him since Tuesday—no, no, much worse—— Jim's dead. Yes, dead—— I know, dear, I try to look at it in that light, but it's very very hard—you see, after all he was my husband—— I know three months wasn't long, but still—— You do say divine things—it wasn't very kind of him, was it?—— Well, dear, Maggie and Flossie and I are lunching at Ciro's at one—come too, and we'll talk it all over then. Good-bye.

(*She hangs up receiver and then rings up again.*)

Hallo, hallo, Exchange—— Mayfair 6773, please—yes—— Hallo, is that the Guards' Club—yes, put me through to Lieutenant Godalming, please—yes, please—— (*She puts receiver down for a moment while she takes puff from under her pillow and powders her nose—then she speaks again.*) Hallo, is that you, darling?—— Oh, I'm sorry, Higgins, I thought it was Lieutenant Godalming—in his bath?—— Please, please get him out of it, Higgins, it's frightfully important—— Yes, I'll hold on—— (*There is a pause.*) Darling—something too fearful has happened—yes, absolutely appalling—Jim's dead. What—who's Jim? He's my husband, of course—yes, he jumped off Waterloo Bridge last night—— *He jumped off Waterloo Bridge last night. No! Waterloo Bridge!* Your ears must be full of soap—— Isn't it dreadful?—— Now, Bobbie dear, you mustn't be naughty—— No, darling, I won't listen to you—I'm very, very miserable—it's been a terrible shock—— Very well, I'll forgive you—— Kiss me, then. (*She responds to his kisses over the telephone.*) Yes, to-night—somewhere quiet—really quiet—I shan't have any appetite—— No, that would be too heartless—— No, that would be too dull—— Say the Embassy—— All right, good-bye, darling—Bobbly wobbly——

(*She hangs up receiver and rings up again.*)

Hallo—— Brixton 8146, please—— Hallo, is that you, Mr. Isaacstein? It's Miss Baker speaking—will you fetch my mother down, please—— Yes, it's important. (*A slight pause.*) Is that you, Mum?—— What do you think, Jim's been and drowned himself—— I don't know—I expect Freda drove him to it—— No, mother, I won't have you saying things like that—besides, he's too young to marry yet—— Look here, Flossie, Violet, Maggie and I are lunching at Ciro's—— One o'clock—come along too and we'll talk it all over—— You can wear that old one of mine—— All right.

(*She rings off and screams for her* MAID.)

Lily—Lilee—come here——

(*She pushes breakfast-tray to the end of the bed and is just about to spring out when her* MAID *enters, sobbing bitterly.*)

What is it?—— What's the matter with you?

LILY. It's dreadful, dreadful——

POPPY. What's dreadful?

LILY. That poor dear upstairs——

POPPY. Mrs. Straker?

LILY. Yes, Mrs. Straker—she's just heard that her husband jumped off Waterloo Bridge last night.

POPPY. What!!

(*The telephone rings violently.* POPPY *snatches up the receiver, listens for a moment, then hurls the instrument to the floor.*)

(*Through clenched teeth.*) Sorry you've been troubled!

BLACK OUT

## "RAIN BEFORE SEVEN——"

1922

CHARACTERS :

TOM
MARY

*The Scene is a private sitting-room in an extremely luxurious hotel in Venice. There is an open window at the back looking on to the Grand Canal, from which comes the occasional hooting of steam-launches and the intermittent sound of someone singing to a guitar across the water. The sun streams in, illuminating an attractively prepared breakfast table, placed exactly in front of the window. There are two doors, one on each side of the room.*

(TOM *enters from the left, attired in a dressing-gown and pyjamas. He goes across to the opposite door and knocks upon it.*)

TOM. Hurry up.
MARY (*inside*). Coming.

(TOM *goes rather moodily to the window and stares out. Enter* MARY *in an enchanting negligee; she goes up to* TOM *and shakes hands.*)

MARY. Good morning, Tom dear; are there any letters?

TOM. I forgot to look.

MARY. You always do. (*She sits down at table.*) Here they are—two for me.

TOM (*also sitting down*). Do pour out the coffee before you open them; I'm dying of thirst.

MARY (*pleasantly*). A little crotchety this morning. (*She begins to pour out coffee.*)

TOM. Not at all, but as breakfast's already been waiting a half an hour——

MARY. *How* you exaggerate!—Here you are—— (*She hands him coffee and then opens a letter.*) This is from Freda Mainwaring.

TOM. What fun.

MARY. You used to like her.

TOM. I never said I didn't.

MARY. Have some grape-fruit, dear—it's cooling.

(*There is silence for a moment.*)

She says she envies us terribly, spending our honeymoon in Venice, in the middle of such beauty, and romance, and everything——

TOM. If she only knew.

MARY. If she only knew what?

TOM. How different we're being.

MARY. She'd envy us more than ever, because she'd

realise that we have the best thing of all—Real companionship.

TOM. Yes, real companionship without sex. It's a marvellous achievement; I can't imagine why no one ever thought of it before, it's so sound—through and through——!

MARY. So many marriages have been ruined by people not being careful enough of their happiness.

TOM. Passion is such a terribly destroying thing. Once you let go it burns and burns until everything is consumed utterly, and then you have to grope among the dead ashes to find a little affection and comradeship, and it's generally too late.

MARY. I can't help feeling awfully proud of the way we're managing *our* lives—here we are in Venice together and it's perfect—much more perfect without ragged edges and cheap sentiment—we've got peace, and above everything else—Freedom.

TOM. And all because we're exercising a little control and mental balance—— I should like some toast, please.

MARY. Here you are—it's quite brittle, like china.

TOM (*taking toast*). Thanks—— And it's so lovely to think that later on, when we know one another thoroughly and have grown to understand one another's every mood—then——

MARY. Then our real honeymoon—— (*She sighs.*) Ah!

TOM (*also sighing*). Ah!—— Pass the marmalade.

MARY. Did you sleep well?

TOM. Beautifully. Did you?

MARY. Yes. I read for a couple of hours before I dropped off.

TOM. So did I.

MARY. There was someone singing across the canal.

TOM (*gloomily*). There always is.

MARY. I'm beginning to know you awfully well already.

TOM (*with his mouth full*). Good.

MARY. Yes, the real you, not the bridegroom you.

TOM. I'm beginning to appreciate you, too, much more than at first.

MARY (*demurely*). Perhaps at the end of six months we shall be so sure of each other that it won't be necessary to wait the whole year until we——

TOM (*dreamily*). Until we—— More coffee, please.

MARY. Do you remember that couple drifting along in the gondola last night?

TOM. Damned fools!

MARY. Stupid sentimentalists.

TOM. Still, they did look happy.

MARY. They looked very silly.

TOM. Where shall we lunch?

MARY. The Lido; then we can bathe.

TOM. I don't like bathing in front of all those people.

MARY. I'm sure they'd look away if you asked them nicely.

TOM. Don't be sarcastic.

MARY. I'm not; only everything I suggest you find fault with.

TOM. You're always so petulant in the early morning —I detest petulance.

MARY (*bitterly*). If you confined *your* unpleasant habits to the early morning I could bear them better——

TOM. This was how the row started yesterday.

MARY (*vehemently*). *And* the day before, *and* the day before that! We've been married exactly a week and we've had a sordid squabble every day.

TOM. On Tuesday we had two.

MARY. Well, it's nothing to boast of.

TOM (*with fearful calmness*). Mary *dear*, you won't be irritating any more, will you, because I don't think I can cope with it.

MARY. Me irritating! I like that, I *must* say. You've been surly and disagreeable ever since breakfast.

TOM. I haven't been anything of the sort.

MARY. Must you go on drumming your spoon against your saucer? It isn't exactly an *aid* to conversation.

TOM (*gently and furiously*). Damn, damn, damn! (*He bangs his saucer with the spoon and breaks it.*)

MARY (*triumphantly*). There now.

TOM. If you racked your brains for hours you couldn't find a more utterly pointless remark than "There now."

MARY (*bitingly*). I find it exceedingly difficult to keep up to the level of your brilliant intelligence.

TOM. Obviously.

MARY (*rising, furiously*). Oh! (*She catches her sleeve in the milk jug and upsets it.*)

TOM. There now.

MARY (*with ominous calm*). Tom, there are moments when I find you quite insufferable.

TOM. Thank you. That was one of your grand

remarks. You are exceedingly funny when you're grand.

MARY. Funny, am I? Huh!

TOM. Yes, extremely—— Ha! ha! ha! (*He drums his spoon against his cup.*)

MARY. You're drumming again.

TOM. I'll drum as much as ever I like. (*He breaks cup.*)

BOTH. There now.

MARY. Control yourself.

TOM. Control! I defy the Archangel Gabriel to control himself on a honeymoon with you.

MARY. As there is not the least likelihood of my spending a honeymoon with the Archangel Gabriel it seems useless to pursue the subject.

TOM. You're trying to be clever and it's obviously a bitter strain.

MARY. All I can say is—thank God I was clever enough to persuade you to carry out our experiment——

TOM (*losing all control*). *You* clever enough! the idea was *entirely* mine.

MARY (*bursting into tears*). I didn't realise I was marrying a liar as well as a brute——

TOM. Now cry—go on—cry.

MARY. I am crying.

TOM. Well, stop then.

MARY. Thank heaven we're not really married.

TOM. We are.

MARY. I mean properly.

TOM. Don't be disgusting.

MARY. Oh, I hate you—I hate you! And I could go

on my knees in thankfulness that I've found you out before it was too late——

TOM. Why must we go on quarrelling like this—why, why, why?

MARY. If you expect to find a solution by shouting you'll be disappointed.

TOM. Experiment! A damn successful experiment this has been. I'm as thankful as you are that we're only tied legally, not morally—at least there *is* a way out.

MARY (*sobbing*). Divorce, as soon as possible.

TOM. If you don't stop crying it will be murder.

MARY (*screaming*). Oh, you beast—you beast! . . .

(*They both rush into their separate rooms and bang the doors—there is a silence for a moment—the voice of a singing* GONDOLIER *draws near and passes the window—a sugar-sweet love song.* MARY *comes quietly out of her room sniffing a little. She goes across to* TOM'S *door and is about to knock when a thought strikes her. She takes the box of cigarettes from the table and empties them all into a vase, then she bangs on his door.*)

TOM. What is it?

MARY (*in a stifled voice*). There aren't any cigarettes—I want some.

(TOM *after a moment gives her a handful of cigarettes round the door and then shuts it again firmly. She lifts her hand to knock again, then looks down at the cigarettes she is holding, then with a little cry of rage she throws them out of the window and stamps back into her room. There is a moment's pause, then* TOM *comes out of his room—he has an unlighted cigarette in his mouth—he goes to the table, picks up a match-box, strikes a match; as he is about to light his cigarette he pauses, thinking, until the match burns his finger. Then he puts the match-box into the vase and starts as his fingers encounter the cigarettes. He brings out a handful and stares at them thoughtfully for a moment, then looks towards her door. A slow smile dawns over his face, he puts the cigarettes back into the vase. The clock strikes ten—with a look of determination he whips a silk handkerchief out of his pocket and drapes it over the face of the clock, then walks quietly but firmly into* MARY'S *room, closing the door after him and turning the key in the lock.)*

BLACK OUT

## LOVE, LIFE AND LAUGHTER

1924

### Scene I

Scene: *The exterior of " La Chatte Vierge," Paris.*
Time: 1890.

(*Two elegant Englishmen,* Rupert Shufflebotham *and his friend* Herbert, *enter.*)

Herbert. This is a very dangerous quarter, Rupert.

Rupert. Nevertheless, it is the place for which we have been searching—see " La Chatte Vierge."

Herbert. Ah, Rupert, sometimes I cannot help but feel that your headstrong impetuosity will one day lead you into a scrape from which you will find it difficult to extricate yourself.

Rupert. Shhh, someone approaches——

(*A* Woman *slouches across.*)

Herbert. Have a care, Rupert, she is a creature of the night.

Rupert. Pauvre petite! These women, Herbert, painted shadows of a great city. Nocturnal butterflies living for an hour and then—pshaw—they are gone.

Herbert. You display too much interest in these

unfortunates; it is, after all, merely to see the queen of them all that we are here.

RUPERT. She has beckoned me from every nook and cranny of Paris, she has tortured my imagination—I must see her—come—let us enter——

(*They go into the café.*)

## SCENE II

*The Scene is a café in Montmartre, "La Chatte Vierge."*
TIME: *Period about* 1890.

(*When the curtain rises several couples are dancing with slightly forced abandon.* MADAME CRAPOTTE, *the proprietress, is seated at a high desk.*)

(*After a time two elegant* ENGLISHMEN *enter in the costume of the period.* RUPERT *is the more elaborately dressed of the two—he also wears Dundreary whiskers.*)

MADAME. Bon soir, Monsieur.

RUPERT. So this is La Chatte Vierge.

MADAME. The only one in Paris, Monsieur.

RUPERT. Come, Herbert, cast aside your melancholy air and let us order some wine.

(*They sit down at a table.*)

HERBERT. You're mad, Rupert. This place has an evil reputation.

RUPERT. A fig for your scruples. Garçon, bring champagne.

WAITER. Bien, Monsieur.

(*The* WAITER *goes to the bar, gets champagne and puts it on the table.*)

HERBERT. Why have you dragged me here?

RUPERT. You ask me that? You know me, Herbert. I am young, I want life. I have come to see La Flamme.

HERBERT (*anxiously*). Shhhhh . . . not so loudly.

RUPERT. I have seen her so often in the distance. Notre Dame, the Louvre, Versailles, the Moulin Rouge, the Morgue.

HERBERT (*gloomily*). She is a bad, bad woman, Rupert.

RUPERT. A bad woman? What of that if she is good company.

HERBERT (*rises*). I for one will be no partner to your crazy scheme.

RUPERT (*rises, and puts his hand on* HERBERT'S *shoulder*). The thought of her sends the blood coursing through my veins like one o'clock.

HERBERT. I shall leave you.

RUPERT. It ill becomes one of the Worcestershire Framptons to show the white feather. (*Sits.*)

HERBERT. Shh . . . Here she is.

(*Enter* LA FLAMME.)

(*Everyone stops dancing. She is attired in a glittering sequin dress, an enormous hat and long black gloves.* HERBERT *takes his leave of* RUPERT *and—goes out.*)

(LA FLAMME *after a bold look round seats herself at a table on the opposite side of the stage from* RUPERT *and beckons* MADAME CRAPOTTE *imperiously.*)

HERBERT. Hoity toity !

LA FLAMME (*to* MADAME CRAPOTTE). Dîtes moi. Qui est cet homme dégoûtant là ?

MADAME. An Englishman—very rich, with estates all over Shropshire.

LA FLAMME (*laughing merrily*). La la la la la ! Nom de Gare du Nord—bring me some absinthe.

(*The* WAITER *brings bottle of absinthe. She pours some out—smiles alluringly across at* RUPERT *and raises her glass to him. She then beckons to him and he rises and comes over to her.*)

Vous êtes Anglais, my fren' ?

RUPERT. Oui, oui, I am.

LA FLAMME. You speak French like a native. Sit down.

RUPERT (*sitting down*). God forgive me—but you are wonderful.

LA FLAMME. They call me La Flamme because I make men mad. What is your name ?

RUPERT. Shufflebotham.

LA FLAMME. La la la la la la ! But they are droll, these English—Shooflebotaam. Tu es séduisant. We will be 'ow you say ?—The good fren's, hein ?

RUPERT. You beautiful white devil.

LA FLAMME. Absinthe, more absinthe. (*She pours out absinthe for them both.*) A toast, my little Shooflebotaam. (*Rises.*) I drink to love—the love of a day—the love of a night—the love of an hour. Les fleurs du mal. (*Gives him glass and sits.*)

RUPERT (*in terrible French*). Mon Dieu—comme vous êtes ravisante. You intoxicate me. I want to crush you in my arms—to smother you with red hot kisses from top to toe. Teach me to love.

LA FLAMME. Have a care, bold cabbage.

(DUET: LA FLAMME and RUPERT)

Hark to the music enthralling, appalling,
It dies away, and then——

RUPERT.

Women like you, so inviting, exciting,
Play fast and loose with men.
Fate has smiled on our meeting,
Feel my pulse madly beating.

LA FLAMME.

Call for more drinks
This is what the world thinks
Is La Vie Parisienne.

BOTH.

Love, life and laughter
Ta - re - da - re - da comes after.

RUPERT.

Hearts are on fire
With the flame of desire.

LA FLAMME.

Lovers surrender
Regardless of gender.
Away care and sorrow,
Never worry about to-morrow.

BOTH.

We will rule passion's kingdom for a day,
For that's the Bohemian way.

RUPERT.

Teach me the bliss of profanity's kiss
As we sway beneath the moon.

LA FLAMME.

Lovers may sip
Passion's wine from my lip
To a gay romantic tune.

RUPERT.

Cupid's dart has impaled me,
All my breeding has failed me,
I want to smite you and beat you and bite you
And swoon and swoon and swoon.

BOTH.

Love, life and laughter
To the devil with what comes after.

RUPERT.

Here is my heart, you can tear it apart,
Nothing suffices but decadent vices

BOTH.

And mirth, folly, madness,
Never giving a thought to sadness.

LA FLAMME.

If you told me to die I should obey.

BOTH.

For that's just the Bohemian way.

(DANCE)

# FÊTE GALANTE

## 1923

### (Preliminary Announcement)

Ladies and Gentlemen, there can be no doubt that as a nation we possess many sterling qualities. But there is unfortunately one slight criticism invariably uttered by any foreigner visiting our island. We are accused of taking our pleasures sadly. This to the outside observer must appear to be regrettably true. We feel, therefore, that it would be interesting to take a perfectly commonplace institution typical of English country life, such as a vicarage garden party, and treat it in the truly effervescent musical comedy spirit.

(*The Scene is a charming English garden. On the R. is a netted-in tennis court, against which balls bounce occasionally. There is, on the L., a terrace, and then the vicarage itself. The sun is shining and Nature appears really at its best. The only things that slightly mar the general summer radiance are the peculiar and rather drab clothes of the garden party guests.*)

(*When the curtain rises* EVERYONE *is strolling backwards and forwards and chatting vivaciously. They* ALL *burst into an enthusiastic Opening Chorus.*)

(OPENING CHORUS)

"*Raspberry Time in Runcorn*"

CHORUS.

When it's raspberry time in Runcorn,
  In Runcorn, in Runcorn,
The air is like a draught of wine,
The undertaker cleans his sign,
The Hull express goes off the line,
When it's raspberry time in Runcorn.

SOLO.

The happy-hearted rural Dean—

CHORUS.

  In Runcorn, in Runcorn—

SOLO.

Plays cricket on the village green

CHORUS.

  In Runcorn, in Runcorn.

SOLO.

And as before the vestry door
  With cricket bat he poises,
From far and near you always hear
  The most peculiar noises.

CHORUS.

For it's raspberry time, raspberry time, raspberry
  time in Runcorn.

(*Four* SPINSTERS *in extremely drab clothes step brightly forward.*)

SPINSTERS.

We're little Parish workers,
With indefinite desires,
Determined to improve the shining hour.
Though years of firm repression
May have quenched our inward fires,
Undoubtedly we've turned a tri-fle sour.
We're busy little beavers,
And we decorate the Church.
Our moral standard's very, very high.
The flower of English manhood
May have left us in the lurch
But we know we'll go to Heaven when we die.

CHORUS.

Ha ! ha ! ha ! Ha ! ha ! ha !
It's raspberry time in Runcorn,
Ho ! ho ! ho ! Ho ! ho ! ho !
It's raspberry time in Runcorn.

(*Six* LITTLE BOYS *in dreadful suits detach themselves from the crowd.*)

BOYS.

We're six dirty little choir boys
With really frightful minds,
We scream and shout and rush about
And pinch our friends' behinds.
Nobody could admire boys
With dirty hands and knees,

But the countryside rejoices
At our sweet soprano voices,
So we do what we damn well please.

CHORUS.
Raspberry time, raspberry time.
Oh ! it's raspberry time in Runcorn.

1ST GIRL. Here comes Nellie Hodgson.
2ND GIRL. She really is as pretty as a picture.
3RD GIRL. All the men are wild about her.

(*Enter* NELLIE *vivaciously. She is dressed in a strawberry pink dress, with a sash and white cotton stockings and gloves. Her hat has a lot of cornflowers all over it and is well on the back of her head.*)

NELLIE. Hullo, everybody, have you heard the news ?
1ST GIRL. No, no ; tell us, Nellie.
NELLIE. I'm engaged to be married, at last.
2ND GIRL. Hurray, hurray, how lovely !
NELLIE. To the curate !
3RD GIRL. There'll be high jinks at the vicarage, I'll be bound.

(SONG : NELLIE : "*The Vicarage Dance*")

I

NELLIE.
I'm just seventeen and a rogue of a girl ;
My heart is a-throbbing with carnival's whirl.
Lovers in plenty I'll have before dawn,
As I dance in my semi of mercerised lawn !

(*Refrain*)

Come with me, come to the vicarage dance.
Quick to the Ball we must hasten.
Those who have gout are allowed to sit out
Under the Lavatory Basin.
Several old deans behind Japanese screens
Give naughty Cupid a chance,
Though I get cramp I'm no end of a scamp
Down at the vicarage dance.

(*She dances with the* CHORUS *and—Exits.*)

(*Enter the* CURATE *and the* VICAR.)

(EVERYONE *clusters round them.*)

1ST GIRL. Congratulations on your engagement, Mr. Spout.

CURATE. Thank you, thank you a thousand times.

VICAR. Ah! well, youth will be served. I remember just before I married I . . .

2ND GIRL. Oh! do tell us!

VICAR. No, no. This is neither the time nor the place.

3RD GIRL. Isn't it awfully dull sometimes to be a clergyman?

CURATE. Even we have our moments.

(*The* CHORUS *rush off.*)

(DUET: CURATE AND VICAR)

*"Even Clergymen are Naughty Now and Then"*

I

CURATE.

People have a wrong idea of Members of the Cloth;
It's really an enjoyable profession.
And though we don't indulge in much frivolity and froth,
We really haven't cause for much depression.
Our lives are full of jollity and gaiety and fun.
With christenings and funerals and such
There's not a week goes by
In which someone doesn't die,
So we really mustn't grumble very much.

(*Refrain*)

BOTH.

When we wake up in the morning and the birds are trilling,
There is something thrilling
In the air;

CURATE.

I can feel my pulses starting
As I struggle with my parting,
And my thoughts go gaily darting
Here and there.

BOTH.

When we visit village invalids on New Year's Day
We're really just as gay
As other men;

VICAR.
Mrs. Jones, whom I was chaffing,
Had a fit and died from laughing;

BOTH.
Even clergymen are naughty
Now and then.

2

VICAR.
The villagers will never disregard a festive cause,
To join in any jumble sale or raffle,
And every Christmas evening I appear as Santa Claus,
A good disguise which never fails to baffle.
A whist drive in the Parish Room
Could only be described
As a positively brilliant affair.
And when old Mrs. Meyer
Gives a picnic for the choir
It's really almost more than we can bear.

*Refrain*

BOTH.
When we wake up in the morning and the weather's bad
We're really always glad
To be alive.

VICAR.
With a faithful repetition
Of our family tradition
Every year a new edition
Will arrive.

BOTH.
Though we fill the cup of duty to the very brim

Ideas may sometimes swim
  Into our ken.

CURATE.
When our thoughts are most volcanic
We remember in our panic
Even clergymen are naughty
  Now and then.

(THEY *execute a short dance and—go off.*)

(*The* CHORUS *rush on again for the Finale, which is sung by the* VICAR'S WIFE *with great verve and dash.*)

FINALE

*"Church Parade"*

VICAR'S WIFE.
On every Sunday morning
  See the righteous leave their houses,
With perching hats adorning,
  Feather boas and dressy blouses,
Their souls devoid of base emotions,
They're on their way to their devotions.

*Refrain*

Church parade, church parade;
See the different types displayed—
Tall ones, short ones, thin and stout,
Everyone looking quite aggressively devout.
Church parade, church parade,
Truculent and undismayed,

There's Mrs. Bowls in grey sateen,
Her hat's the queerest shape I can remember having
seen,
It makes me quite suspicious as to what it might have
been.
Oh, Church Parade.

*2nd Refrain*

Church parade, church parade,
See the different types portrayed.
Christian women, large and small,
With nothing in their faces to distinguish them at all.
Church parade, church parade,
Truculent and undismayed,
Those young ladies don't read Freud,
Their virginal mentalities are otherwise employed;
Maybe that's the reason that they look so unenjoyed.
Oh, Church parade!

# TRAVELLING LIGHT

1924

## CHARACTERS:

A Young Woman
A Young Man
A Wagon-Lit Attendant

(*The scene is a compartment in the Orient Express. On the R. side is the sliding door, opening into the corridor, and in the right the window. The two corner seats have reserved notices pinned over them. The* Attendant *ushers in the* Young Woman *and places her bag in the rack.* Attendant *goes L.*)

Woman. Is there anyone else in this carriage?

Attendant. Yes, Madame, a young gentleman. He is in the restaurant.

(*The train gives a sudden jerk and starts.*)

Woman. I thought we waited here longer than that.

Attendant. No, Madame; only quarter of an hour.

Woman. Look here, Attendant. Are there no sleepers vacant?

ATTENDANT. No, Madame; not until we get to the frontier.

WOMAN. When will that be?

ATTENDANT. About half-past two.

WOMAN. You'd better reserve me one, then.

ATTENDANT. Very well, Madame.

WOMAN. Unfortunately, I've had my handbag stolen, so I shall not be able to pay for it until we arrive at Trieste. My friends are meeting me there.

ATTENDANT. Very sorry, Madame, but you can't have a sleeper unless you pay in advance. That's one of the company's rules.

WOMAN. Could you break it? Just this once.

ATTENDANT. I'm afraid not.

WOMAN. But I tell you, my friends are meeting me at Trieste. They'll settle up with you.

ATTENDANT. I'm sorry, Madame; it's out of the question.

WOMAN. But this is outrageous; surely you can trust me!

ATTENDANT. The company's orders are "not to trust anyone."

WOMAN. I'll make it worth your while.

ATTENDANT. It's no good, Madame, I can't do it.

WOMAN. Well, all I can say is, it's disgusting. I've travelled by this route hundreds of times, and now because I have the misfortune to lose my bag, I am treated as though I were a suspicious character.

ATTENDANT. Anyone who loses their bag is a suspicious character, Madame; that's another of the company's rules.

WOMAN. Please don't be impertinent.

ATTENDANT. I'm sorry, Madame.

WOMAN. I haven't even got any change; I shan't be able to have so much as a cup of coffee.

ATTENDANT. I wouldn't mind standing you a cup of coffee.

WOMAN. Kindly go away, and don't be familiar.

ATTENDANT. Certainly, Madame. I hope you'll spend a comfortable night.

WOMAN (*angrily*). Oh!

(*The* ATTENDANT *withdraws; the* WOMAN *opens an attaché case. Just as she is settling herself, the* YOUNG MAN *enters.*)

YOUNG MAN (*stepping over her feet*). Excuse me.

WOMAN. I'm sorry. (*She tucks her legs under the seat.*)

(*The* YOUNG MAN *sits down in his corner, they both observe one another covertly for a little while.*)

YOUNG MAN. Do you mind if I smoke?

WOMAN. Not at all.

YOUNG MAN (*producing cigarette-case*). Perhaps you'd like one?

WOMAN. Oh, thank you so much. (*She takes one and he lights them.*) I'm in an absolute fury.

YOUNG MAN. Why?

WOMAN. There aren't any sleepers vacant.

YOUNG MAN. I know. It's frightfully annoying. The man said there might be some going at the frontier. I'm only going as far as Milan, so it wouldn't really be worth it.

WOMAN. It's all very badly arranged.

YOUNG MAN. Yes. The only thing is to make ourselves as comfortable as possible here.

WOMAN. Yes ! I suppose it is !

(*There is silence.*)

YOUNG MAN (*peering out of the window*). I think it has started to rain.

WOMAN. How lovely !

YOUNG MAN. I say, don't snap at me !

WOMAN. I warned you that I was cross.

YOUNG MAN. Yes, but not with me !

WOMAN. Not yet.

YOUNG MAN. Oh !

(*There is another silence.*)

I didn't see you in the Restaurant Car.

WOMAN. I've only just got in.

YOUNG MAN. I loathe dining on the train, anyhow.

WOMAN. I haven't dined at all.

YOUNG MAN. Oh, I say ! Why not ?

WOMAN. I hadn't got any . . . time.

YOUNG MAN. Look here, I've got a little food and some champagne. Will you have it ?

WOMAN. Oh ! really, I couldn't.

YOUNG MAN. Oh ! please do. It will only be wasted if you don't.

WOMAN. It's extremely kind of you.

(*He gets hamper down from the rack and opens it. Then he serves her with some chicken and salad on a paper plate.*)

How delicious ! It really is charming of you.

YOUNG MAN. I'll open the bottle.

WOMAN. Do be careful. I'm terrified of champagne corks.

YOUNG MAN. They are rather violent, aren't they. (*He opens it successfully.*)

WOMAN. Yes, they are. You must have some too.

YOUNG MAN. There's only one glass.

WOMAN. Never mind, we'll share it. (*He pours out a glassful.*)

YOUNG MAN. You first.

WOMAN. Yes! (*Drinking some and handing it back.*) Now you.

YOUNG MAN (*drinking*). Thanks. This is rather fun, isn't it?

WOMAN. You're saving my life and my temper.

YOUNG MAN. Have some more.

WOMAN. Yes. (*She has some more.*)

YOUNG MAN. Is that chicken all right?

WOMAN. Perfect.

YOUNG MAN. Good.

(*There is a silence.*)

How's the salad?

WOMAN. Divine.

YOUNG MAN. It looks rather old.

WOMAN. I prefer it old.

YOUNG MAN. Have some more champagne.

WOMAN. All right. I hope it won't go to my head.

YOUNG MAN. I hope it will. (*He pours out some more.*)

WOMAN. That was very naughty of you.

YOUNG MAN. Here.

WOMAN. No, you first this time.

YOUNG MAN. Righto ! (*He drinks some.*) Now you.

WOMAN. Thank you. I drink to your health, wealth and happiness.

YOUNG MAN (*bowing*). I possess two of those quantities at the present moment. (*Sits again.*)

WOMAN. I'm so glad. There now, I've eaten enormously.

YOUNG MAN. Allow me. (*He takes her plate and puts it back in the basket.*) There's some very sombre looking cake and an apple.

WOMAN. No more, thank you.

YOUNG MAN. Sure.

WOMAN. Positive.

YOUNG MAN. We'll put the hamper away, then. All except the champagne.

WOMAN. You must put that away, too. I couldn't drink any more.

YOUNG MAN (*putting hamper back on rack*). Nonsense, there's a lot left.

WOMAN. I'm afraid it couldn't have been an ordinary sized bottle.

YOUNG MAN (*handing her glass*). Here.

WOMAN. No, no : really !

YOUNG MAN. Come along. Please, just a little.

WOMAN. Only a sip, then. (*She spills a few drops.*)

YOUNG MAN. Oh ! that's lucky ! Permit me. (*He wets his fingers in the wine and rubs some behind her ears.*)

WOMAN. Oh ! you're tickling me. You must have some too. (*She does the same.*) For luck. (*Bus. Gives him cup.*)

YOUNG MAN. Won't you take off your hat ?

WOMAN. Shall I ?

YOUNG MAN. It would be cosier.

WOMAN. Very well. (*She does so and fluffs out her hair before the glass.*) There . . .

YOUNG MAN. What pretty hair !

WOMAN. Sh ! Tut ! Tut ! You mustn't say things like that.

YOUNG MAN. Why not, if I'm sincere ?

WOMAN. Are you ?

YOUNG MAN. Damnably.

(*There is a slight pause, while they gaze into each other's eyes.*)

WOMAN. Yes !

YOUNG MAN. Let's finish the champagne.

WOMAN. Very well.

YOUNG MAN (*pouring it out*). You first, this time.

WOMAN. Yes. (*She drinks.*) Now you.

(YOUNG MAN *looking into her eyes, he turns the glass round and drinks from where she has drunk. She looks down.*)

WOMAN. Please may I have another cigarette. (*Pause . . . repeat.*)

YOUNG MAN. Oh yes, of course !

(*He lights fresh cigarette for her.*)

WOMAN. I suppose we'd better try to sleep a little.

YOUNG MAN. Yes, I suppose we had. (*Puts coat over himself.*)

WOMAN. Would you think it dreadful of me if I took off my shoes ?

YOUNG MAN. Lord, no ! Let me help you.

WOMAN. No, please not. (*She kicks them off.*)

YOUNG MAN. Won't you have a rug.

WOMAN. No, really, thank you !

YOUNG MAN. I insist ; I have my overcoat.

(*She tucks her feet up and he wraps the rug round her.*)

WOMAN. You're being most frightfully sweet to me, and I am so, so grateful.

YOUNG MAN. If you only knew what a pleasure it was. (*Sits.*) Shall we turn out the light or keep it on ?

WOMAN. Leave it on. (*Bus.*) Put it out.

(*He turns out the light.*)

(*In the darkness the two glowing cigarette-ends appear to draw closer and closer to each other ; when they meet the curtain falls. It rises again in a moment or two. A few hours have elapsed. The* YOUNG MAN *is asleep and snoring. The* YOUNG WOMAN *is putting on her shoes. The* ATTENDANT *enters.*)

ATTENDANT. You rang, Madame ?

WOMAN. Shh ! He's asleep.

ATTENDANT. Very human, Madame. Life's like that.

WOMAN. When do we reach the frontier ?

ATTENDANT. In about ten minutes.

WOMAN (*handing him some money*). I find I shall be able to pay for that sleeper after all.

ATTENDANT (*taking it*). Life's like that, Madame.

BLACK OUT

# FIRST LOVE

1924

## CHARACTERS:

EFFIE
RUPERT
MADEMOISELLE

SCENE: *Schoolroom.*

(RUPERT *and* EFFIE *are seated one at each side of the table, studying.*)

EFFIE (*monotonously to herself*). J'aime, tu aime, il aime, nous aimons.

RUPERT. Effie!

EFFIE. Je voie, tu voies, il voit. Nous voyons, vous voyez, ils . . .

RUPERT. You're driving me mad! Why can't you keep quiet?

EFFIE. I learn quicker than you; Mademoiselle said so.

RUPERT. She didn't.

EFFIE. She did.

RUPERT. You're a liar!

EFFIE. Ask her.

RUPERT. Oh, shut up !

EFFIE (*after a pause*). Avez-vous vu le vieux hibou sur la haie ?

RUPERT. I shouldn't mind so much if only you hadn't got adenoids ?

EFFIE (*ignoring him*). Non, mais j'ai vu votre tante hier soir.

RUPERT. Effie !

EFFIE. What ?

RUPERT. Do me a favour.

EFFIE. What is it ?

RUPERT. When Mademoiselle comes, ask to leave the room.

EFFIE. Why ?

RUPERT. It's a very special favour.

EFFIE. I shan't want to.

RUPERT. That doesn't matter ; you can pretend, can't you ?

EFFIE. Yes, but why ?

RUPERT. It's a secret.

EFFIE. Something about me ?

RUPERT. No !

EFFIE (*resuming her studies*). Voulez-vous me donner votre crayon, Alphonse ?

RUPERT. Effie !

EFFIE. What ?

RUPERT. Will you ?

EFFIE. No !

RUPERT. You could say you feel sick !

EFFIE. Why ?

RUPERT. I want to talk to Mademoiselle.

EFFIE. What about ?

RUPERT. Never mind. I'll give you Muriel to put in the hutch with Lord Darnley.

EFFIE. Father says it's better for Muriel to live alone. (*Reciting.*) Joli mois de Mai.

RUPERT (*throwing a book at her*). Disagreeable little beast!

EFFIE (*screaming*). Rupert, I'll tell mother.

(*She throws several books at him ; there is a battle, in the middle of which* MADEMOISELLE *enters.*)

MDLLE. Children, what are you doing?

EFFIE. Rupert threw a book at me and he hurt me. (*She cries loudly.*)

MDLLE. Why did you do that, Rupert?

RUPERT. She will learn her lessons aloud.

EFFIE. It isn't that at all; he's cross because I wouldn't be sick.

MDLLE. Wouldn't be sick?

EFFIE. Yes, so that he could tell you a secret.

RUPERT. Filthy little sneak!

MDLLE. Rupert, what does this mean?

RUPERT. Nothing!

MDLLE. What secret did you want to tell me?

RUPERT. Nothing! (*He buries his head in his arms.*)

MDLLE. Have you learnt your verbs, Effie?

EFFIE. Yes.

MDLLE. Well, go into the library and write them out from memory. I'll hear Rupert's here.

EFFIE. He doesn't know them.

MDLLE. Go along.

EFFIE (*singing blithely*).

" Il ne connais pas ses verbs
Il ne connais pas ses verbs."

MDLLE (*sharply*). Effie !

(EFFIE *goes out, first of all making a grimace at* RUPERT.)

Rupert, what's the matter ?

RUPERT. Nothing.

MDLLE. Do you know your verbs ?

RUPERT. Only one.

MDLLE. Which one ?

RUPERT (*looking up*). Je t'aime.

MDLLE. I thought that was it.

RUPERT. You knew all the time ?

MDLLE. I guessed, silly boy.

RUPERT. It's not silly ; it's the most wonderful thing in the world . . . love !

MDLLE. First love.

NUMBER

*Verse* 1

HE.

If you could only realise
And knew how I idealised
The very slightest thing you say or do,

SHE.

I've guessed and felt a little bit
Depressed because I know that it
Leads to complications.
Think of your relations'
Point of view.

*Refrain 1*

HE.

First love,
Completely unrehearsed love,
Has all the spontaneity of youth.

SHE.

Well, to tell the truth
I am quite unversed, love,
In treating suitably these adolescent scenes.
You're indisputably the victim of your teens.
New love
Must always seem the true love.
Experience will teach you as you go
Till you really know
Just the way to woo, love.

HE.

I wish you'd show me how my passion should
be nursed,

SHE.

Your Papa will have to raise my wages first,
love.

*Verse 2*

HE.

I've burned to kiss your darling hand,
And yearned to make you understand,
That you're the only one in life for me ;

SHE.

I fear I can't reciprocate,
But, dear, I do appreciate
Having made you suffer.
Darling little duffer,
You'll soon see.

*Refrain 2*

SHE.

First love
Is generally the worst love

HE.

I'm trying to restrain it all the time.
I've a feeling I'm
Really going to burst, love.

SHE.

I fully realise your true romantic soul,
But you must utilise a little self-control.

HE.

Calf love is never half and half love ;
To me you're just the fairest of your sex.
How I love you !

SHE.

Ex—cuse me if I laugh, love,

HE.

Let's plunge in passion till we're totally immersed.

SHE.

I shall have to ask my husband first, love.

## THE TOUCH OF A WOMAN'S HAND

1925

*Verse* 1

EVER since the world began
Woman's been the slave of man;
Years of hard experience have taught her
To be led quite meekly to the slaughter.
But, in quite a subtle way,
She has learnt the game to play.
Gently persevering through the ages,
She has left her mark on history's pages.

*Refrain* 1

Just the touch of a woman's hand
Was ignored when the world was planned,
Why the Tree of Good and Evil should be firmly
shunned,
Eve could never understand.
So she fell for the serpent's hiss,
And surrendered to love's first kiss,
Thus the primitive emotions to a blaze were fanned
By the touch of a woman's hand.

*Verse 2*

Since that early marriage scene,
Centuries have rolled between ;
Husbands of remarkable complacence
Flourished in the days of the Renaissance.
People never tried divorce
When their love had run its course.
If a husband bored his wife completely
She'd prepare his dinner very neatly.

*Refrain 2*

Just the touch of a woman's hand,
Lent a charm to each costly viand,
With the very blissful knowledge that she'd bribed
  her cook,
She'd contrive to look quite bland.
If with some little charming speech
She would help him to half a peach,
He'd be painfully transported to a better land
By the touch of a woman's hand.

*Verse 3*

Girls of the domestic kind
Nowadays are hard to find,
Hearths and homes are violently changing,
Women have a craze for rearranging.
Happy little homes are few,
Politics have claimed their due,
Wives who try to regulate the nations
Devastate their conjugal relations.

*Refrain 3*

Just the touch of a woman's hand
Is improving the Motherland,
For the women politicians have a nasty gift
Of detecting shifting sand.
It would shatter the Empire's hopes
If we listened to Marie Stopes.
All the crèches in the country would at once disband
By the touch of a woman's hand.

## POOR LITTLE RICH GIRL

1925

*Verse 1*

You're only a baby,<br>
You're lonely, and maybe<br>
  Someday soon you'll know<br>
The years you are tasting<br>
Are years you are wasting.<br>
  Life is a bitter foe,<br>
With Fate it's no use competing,<br>
Youth is so terribly fleeting ;<br>
By dancing much faster<br>
You're chancing disaster,<br>
  Time alone will show.

*Refrain*

Poor little rich girl,<br>
You're a bewitched girl,<br>
  Better beware !<br>
Laughing at danger,<br>
Virtuous stranger,<br>
  Better take care.<br>
The life you lead sets all your nerves a-jangle,<br>
Your love affairs are in a hopeless tangle.

Though you're a child, dear,
Your life's a wild typhoon,
Cocktails and laughter,
But what comes after?
  Nobody knows.
In lives of leisure,
The craze for pleasure
  Steadily grows.
You're weaving love into a mad jazz pattern,
  Ruled by Pantaloon,
Poor little rich girl,
  Don't drop a stitch too soon.

*Verse 2*

The role you are acting,
The toll is exacting,
  Soon you'll have to pay;
The music of living
You lose in the giving,
  False things soon decay.
These words from me may surprise you,
I've got no right to advise you,
I've known Life too well, dear,
Your own Life must tell, dear,
  Please don't turn away.

*Refrain (repeat)*

(*At the second Refrain the park railings fade away and give place to curtains. The* GIRL *starts to her feet at the sound of a Jazz Band playing. The* YOUNG MAN *comes on and dances with her. Then another* YOUNG MAN *wrenches her away, and then another. She drifts and sways about among them like a leaf. At last the band stops, and she falls. All the* YOUNG MEN *disappear, and once more it is outside the park.* DAISY *lifts her up and leads her off.*)

DAISY (*with her arm round her*). Silly baby. Come with me and we'll find a taxi.

## THE CAFÉ DE LA PAIX

### 1925

### OPENING SCENE (ACT I—SCENE I)

(*It is about* 11.30 *p.m. outside the Café de la Paix. Only two windows of the café can be seen and a revolving glass door in the centre. Silhouettes of people supping are thrown against the windows. Outside there are three rows of tables and chairs, allowing enough space for the passing up and down of people who are constantly promenading. The footlights should represent the kerb. There is a newspaper kiosk on the left of the stage.*)

(*When the curtain rises, there should be a babel of noise ; everybody talking at once, people walking up and down ; a small newsboy shouting and the constant peek-peek of motor-cars.* ALL *the tables are filled with various types of people, drinking coffee and syrups, and there are three or four* WAITERS, *one with large pots of coffee and hot milk. Two young* ENGLISHMEN *in dinner jackets and silk hats stroll languidly on.*)

1ST ENG. God, what a row these foreigners kick up.
2ND ENG. I wish we were in Piccadilly.

(*A typical Parisian* GUIDE *with a long black moustache approaches them.*)

GUIDE. You wish to see something very very curious?

1ST ENG. What?

GUIDE. You come with me, *hein?*

2ND ENG. Where to?

GUIDE. Not far, we take taxi or walk—as you wish.

1ST ENG. I don't want to do either.

GUIDE. I show you lovely girls; they do plastic poses, very amusing.

2ND ENG. God forbid.

GUIDE. You have not seen "Le Tango d'Amour"?

1ST ENG. No, and we don't want to, thanks. Come on, Freddie.

(*They stroll off.*)

(*The* GUIDE *spits and wanders away. Two vivacious* ENGLISH GIRLS *walk along, chatting. They are in day clothes and hats.*)

1ST GIRL. And, my dear, I looked him full in the face and said, "Just because you're in France, don't imagine you can take liberties."

2ND GIRL. My dear, you didn't.

1ST GIRL. My dear, I did.

2ND GIRL. What did he do?

1ST GIRL. He took hold of both my hands suddenly and kissed me.

2ND GIRL. My dear, he didn't.

1ST GIRL. My dear, he did.

(*They go off.*)

(*Two very excited people nearly bump into them*

*—a* MAN *and* WOMAN. *They walk rapidly across, arguing violently.)*

WOMAN. Tais toi, tais toi. En tous cas tu m'as donné rien encore.

MAN (*protestingly*). Mais, chérie, chérie, je vous assure——

WOMAN. Mais voyons, je ne suis pas une femme comme ça, d'ailleurs il n'y a pas le temps——

(*They go off, still arguing.*)

(*An American family stroll on. They are peculiarly but appropriately dressed. They consist of* MRS. HAMMAKER, MR. HAMMAKER, *their eldest son,* HARRY, *their daughter* IRMA. *A party of people vacate one of the front tables, and so they seat themselves.*)

MRS. H. Are we in Paris or Brussels, Harry?

HARRY. What day of the week is it?

IRMA. Thursday.

HARRY. We are in Paris.

MRS. H. Call the garçon, Earl.

MR. H. (*weakly*). Hi, waiter!

IRMA. Isn't it all too darling heavenly. Look at that cute man selling carpets, Pappa.

HARRY (*grandly*). He's always here.

MRS. H. Harry knows his Paris.

MR. H. What the hell's he selling carpets for at this time of night?

HARRY. He's got to make a living somehow.

IRMA. I think he's divine.

(*A drab* WOMAN *approaches them, selling violets. She is singing gustily.*)

Nous avons fait un beau voyage,
Nous avons fait un beau voyage,
Nous arrêtant à tous les pas,
Nous arrêtant à tous les pas,
Buvant du cidre à chaque village,
Cueillant dans les clos des lilas
Cueillant dans les clos des lilas.

IRMA. Pappa, give her fifty cents.

MR. H. Hi, you!

(WOMAN *approaching.*)

WOMAN. Les belles violettes toutes fraîches, toutes fraîches.

(*She attempts to force a large bunch of violets on to* IRMA'S *chest;* IRMA *screams.*)

HARRY. Hi! Allons, allons, vite. Partez.

WOMAN. Ah, Monsieur, ayez pitié de moi. J'attends un petit, peut-être deux si le bon Dieu l'ordonne.

MRS. H. What does she say?

HARRY. Something about having a little something.

MR. H. (*giving her money*). Here you are; go away.

WOMAN (*moving on*). Merci, que Dieu vous bénisse.
Nous avons fait un beau voyage . . .

(MRS. HUBBARD *enters with her daughter* AMY; *they are in typical dressy blouses, cloaks and no hats, they have been to the Opera.*)

MRS. HUBBARD. Let's sit down here, Amy.

AMY. Look at all the people, mother.

MRS. HUBBARD. It's always the same in Paris, dear. I remember just before your father had his operation——

AMY. Oh! Mother, look at that young man.

MRS. HUBBARD. Don't stare, dear, he might accost us.

AMY. What would happen if he did?

MRS. HUBBARD. Sh! Amy, here comes the waiter. Oh—er—garçon, deux cafay o lay.

WAITER. Complet, Madame.

MRS. HUBBARD. Deux cafay o lay.

WAITER. Brioches, Madame?

MRS. HUBBARD (*offended*). Certainly not. Non. Pas de toot.

AMY. What did he say, mother?

MRS. HUBBARD. Nothing for your ears to hear, dear. Oh, I wish we had a man with us.

AMY. What language are those people speaking at the next table?

MRS. HUBBARD. Spanish, I think, dear; or is it American?

(*The two* ENGLISHMEN *have again strolled on. The* GUIDE *again approaches them. The ensuing scene takes place exactly opposite* MRS. HUBBARD'S *table.*)

GUIDE. You wish to buy a postcard?

1ST ENG. Oh, go away.

GUIDE (*showing card under his coat*). Look, very amusing.

2ND ENG. Look here, if you don't leave us alone, I'll call a gendarme.

1ST ENG. (*knocking postcards out of* GUIDE'S *hand*). Come on, let's go and have a drink.

GUIDE (*picking cards up and swearing*). Sacré nom du chien sale tipe. (*He wanders away, having retrieved his postcards ; one has fallen beneath* AMY'S *chair. She picks it up.*)

AMY. Oh ! Mother, *look !*

MRS. HUBBARD. Where are my glasses ? (*She finds them and looks at it.*) Oh ! (*She falls back clutching her heart.*)

AMY. What's the matter ?

MRS. HUBBARD. Oh ! what a turn that gave me—it's the living image of your Auntie Clara.

AMY. Aren't these foreigners awful ?

MRS. HUBBARD. Never mind, dear, we're all made the same, though some more than others.

(*A party of* ENGLISH PEOPLE *come on in evening dress. They slowly saunter across the stage.*)

VIOLET. Reggie, darling, it's much too early to go to Mitchell's.

REGGIE. What about Zellie's ?

FREDA. No, it's always so packed ; you can't call even your corns your own.

JAMES. What about the Jardin ?

VIOLET. I daren't go there, I'm so terrified of being caricatured by Sem. He did poor Lady Trimble as an otter.

FREDA (*languidly*). Why an otter ?

VIOLET. I suppose because she makes such peculiar noises when drinking.

REGGIE. Let's get a taxi and tell him to take us where he likes.

FREDA (*wearily*). The Paris taxi men only know the Moulin Rouge.

VIOLET. I think I shall go to bed.

JAMES. Why did anyone ever call Paris "the gay city"?

FREDA. God knows, dear; only in comparison to New York and London, I expect.

(*They wander off.*)

MRS. HUBBARD. Do you know who that was, Amy?

AMY. No, mother.

MRS. HUBBARD. Lady Violet Edgware; she's been divorced three times.

AMY. Who was the dark one?

MRS. HUBBARD. Lady Freda Mannering. They say her husband beats her dreadfully. I read her life story in the *Girl's Companion*.

AMY. Oh! do look at that man with the beard, isn't he like Uncle Bob?

MRS. HUBBARD. Certainly not, Amy. Whatever your Uncle Bob's failings were, he never tucked his serviette into his dickey.

(*Their conversation is interrupted by the sudden ejection of a young man from the restaurant. He is in rather shabby clothes. He tears himself free from the* COMMISSIONAIRE, *and producing a revolver, shoots it twice into the air. At once there is an uproar.* EVERYONE *rises and talks at once. The* YOUNG MAN *falls down in a picturesque attitude. In the middle of the turmoil the* COSMOPOLITAN LADY *comes out of the restaurant escorted by several immaculate* YOUNG MEN.)

COMMISS. Ah ! Madame, Madame, il meurt, il meurt.

COS. LADY. No, that is the usual thing ; he always does it. He's crazy about me ; take him away.

YOUNG MAN. I say, aren't you rather heartless ?

COS. LADY. Tais-toi, mon petit. Tu ne comprends pas l'amour française. There are more fireworks than in England, but fewer people get burnt.

YOUNG MAN. But he shot himself.

COS. LADY. No, no, he's not hurt at all. Look !

(*She goes over to the* YOUNG MAN *and kisses him. He immediately jumps up and clasps her in his arms, muttering violent endearments. She disentangles herself from his embrace and signs to the* COMMISSIONAIRE, *who drag him away dithering ecstatically.*)

COS. LADY. Call me a taxi.

(*Three of her escort rush down to the floats and proceed to shout for taxis. They run along, pushing one another out of the way. The* COSMOPOLITAN LADY *is accosted by the flower-seller. She gives her some notes. Then she buys two rugs from the rug-seller. The* YOUNG MEN *take charge of them. Suddenly* TWELVE GIRLS *march on, all dressed demurely alike, with an elderly man in attendance. They all salute the* COS. LADY *and form a polite semicircle round her.*)

YOUNG MAN. What on earth is all this ?

COS. LADY. It's a little school I started after seeing L'Ecole des Cocottes. They all come to watch me leave the Restaurant after dining. Such an education for them. (*To the* KEEPER.) Why are you late?

KEEPER. We were delayed, watching Cecile Sorel getting out of her car at the Comedie Française.

COS. LADY. That's not an education, it's a warning.

KEEPER. Three of the elder girls insisted. They said it was most interesting to compare the old-world methods with the new.

COS. LADY. That's a breach of discipline; I must give them an imposition. Ring up the Guaranty Trust and ask for two Chicago Millionaires and a Pittsburg Senator.

1ST GIRL (*rushing forward*). Let us off this time, Madame, please.

COS. LADY. No, it will be good for you. If you wish to be a successful Cosmopolitan, you must learn to take the rough with the smooth.

2ND GIRL. Have a little pity.

COS. LADY. No one ever had any pity on me!

## SONG: "COSMOPOLITAN LADY"

1925

1

When I was quite a little mite of seven,
    I secretly decided on my course,
Though maybe I'm not heading straight for heaven
    I've never put the cart before the horse.

    (She wouldn't do that, of course.)

It's seldom that my joi de vivre forsakes me,
    I frequently succeed where others fail,
And when the day of judgment overtakes me,
    I'll make a very firm appeal for bail.

(She seems successfully to dominate
And utterly control her fate
    We'll follow very firmly in her trail.)

2

The world to me will always be a gamble;
    I don't care if I win or if I lose;
The straight and narrow path is such a scramble
    And such an unattractive life to choose.

(We'd like to be in your shoes.)

I much prefer a flutter at the tables,
I treat my whole existence as a game,
And if I end in sackcloth or in sables,
I shan't have lived for nothing, all the same.

(We're really quite impatient to begin
A life of unassuming sin
And try to reach your pinnacle of fame.)

*1st Refrain*

I'm a Cosmopolitan lady,
With a Cosmopolitan soul.
Every dashing blonde
Of the demi-monde
Starts to quake when I take a stroll.
My past's incredibly shady,
And my future grows more doubtful every day;
Though determined to be pleasant,
I shall utilise the present
In a Cosmopolitan way.

*2nd Refrain*

I'm a Cosmopolitan lady,
With a Cosmopolitan eye;
From Neuilly sur Seine
To the Madeleine,
I am cheered by the passers-by.
Though my past's incredibly shady,
And my future grows more doubtful every day,
When the men by love are blinded,
I try hard to be broad-minded
In a Cosmopolitan way.

*3rd Refrain*

I'm a Cosmopolitan lady,
  With a Cosmopolitan heart;
    And I've lived so long
    Between right and wrong,
  That I can't tell the two apart.
Though my past's incredibly shady,
And my future grows more doubtful every day,
  Though my methods may be breezy,
  I find virtue very easy,
    In the Cosmopolitan way.

## "SHE WAS A GOOD GIRL THEN"

1926

*Verse* 1

I REMEMBER Mary at a very early age,
She was sweet, sweet, sweet as pie,
She was like a fairy who has fallen on Life's stage
And forgotten how to fly.
She was full of charming and alluring little ways,
Her modesty would leave you quite aghast.
Innocence to her was like a cosy little cage,
But alas! those days are past.

*Refrain* 1

Take it from me she was a good girl then,
She was as fragrant as the blooming cyclamen.
If a schoolboy brought her a bunch of flowers
She'd weep for joy for hours.
She was never misled and was always in bed by ten;
Take it from me that child could do no wrong
Though lots of horrible temptations came along.
When her watch was stolen by her sister Nell,
Mary promptly offered her the chain as well.
Take it from me she was a good girl then.

*Verse* 2

Mary growing older was extremely comme-il-faut
And her ignorance was bliss.

No one ever told her all the things a girl should know,
And the reason why was this.
She was unsophisticated, dancing to and fro
She didn't know the value of her charms,
Dwelling in such innocence it only goes to show
That she seldom suffered qualms.

*Refrain 2*

Take it from me she was a good girl then,
Above her bed was hung The Monarch of the Glen.
In the morning she never pulled the blind up
Till she had made her mind up,
And she finished her prayers with a very devout Amen ;
Take it from me she never went too far,
One day a young man took her driving in his car.
Though he drove her straight into a barbed wired fence
She had never fallen in the stricter sense.
Take it from me she was a good girl then.

*Refrain 3*

Take it from me she was a good girl then,
She really hadn't much experience of men.
She would always blush with surprise if teased much,
Give piercing cries if squeezed much,
And she looked on the world as a sort of lion's den.
Take it from me she was as pure as snow,
She seemed to know by instinct just how far to go.
In the morning when she took her cousin Jack his
 morning tea
Neither of them had their lunch till half-past three.
Take it from me she was a good girl then.

*Refrain* 4

Take it from me she was a good girl then,
Peculiar thoughts had never strayed into her ken.
She was never really depressed or humpy,
Maybe her nerves were jumpy,
But she left it at that and took lots of Sanatogen,
Take it from me she was a bit run down.
The doctor looked at her with quite a worried frown,
Then he told her tactfully and firmly
That she needed care,
So she went to Canada and had it there.
Take it from me she was a good girl then.

# ORANGES AND LEMONS

1925

SKETCH

CHARACTERS:

GRACE HUBBARD
VIOLET BANKS
CHARLIE FRENCH
STEPHEN HARRIS

*(The Scene is a bedroom in a Bloomsbury Boarding House. There are two single beds facing each other. A window at back of stage and a dressing-table, complete with duchess set, including hair-tidy, pin-cushions, etc. There is also a washstand with a rose-bespattered toilet set. One incandescent gas-burner with crinkly pink glass shade. A small table beside each bed with candle and matches, etc., on each. There are some Pears' Annual pictures, the frames of which have been decorated with some depressed sprigs of holly. There are also two dusty-coloured paper chains stretched across the room, and in the grate a large pink paper fire-screen ornament. It is New Year's Eve.)*

(GRACE HUBBARD *and* VIOLET BANKS *enter.* GRACE *is somewhere between forty-five and fifty and rather set for maturity. She is wearing what may technically be described as a " dressy blouse " with lots of beads on it and a plain black skirt, rather up in front and down at the back. Her shoes and open-work stockings are very festive.* VIOLET, *on the other hand—though more or less the same age—is distinctly more " skittish." She is angular and fair, dressed in a tea-gown of voluptuous design ; flowers (artificial) on one shoulder. She wears gold-rimmed pince-nez on a chain. Both the ladies are wearing coloured paper caps.* GRACE *turns up the gas which had been turned low.*)

GRACE (*enters door R. Crosses to fireplace, turns up light*). I do think Mrs. Rogers might have given us a fire.

VIOLET (*sits chair C.*). No idea of comfort ; the English are always like that.

GRACE. You're English yourself, aren't you? (*Crosses to bed R.*)

VIOLET (*tittering*). Well, I'm not altogether ; my grandmother was Spanish, and I was nearly always abroad until I married.

GRACE. Is your husband dead?

VIOLET. Oh, yes, quite ; he behaved very badly to me.

GRACE. They're all the same. Do you mind very much if I take this bed? I always sleep on my right side, and I don't like facing the window.

VIOLET. Certainly. I always sleep curled up. My husband nicknamed me " Pixie," you know.

GRACE. Did he?

VIOLET. Yes; he was whimsical, I will say that for him.

GRACE (*sits on bed*). It is funny. Do you know I haven't shared a room with anyone since my eldest sister's funeral?

VIOLET (*rises, crosses to R. of chair C.*). Well, I don't mind confessing, just between our two little selves, that I was very upset when Mrs. Rogers asked me to have another bed put in here. But after all, I said to myself, one mustn't be disagreeable in the middle of so much jollity.

GRACE. Quite, quite. (*Takes hair down.*) Will you wash first, or shall I?

VIOLET (*beginning to undo her dress*). I'll rinse my hands later. I never touch my face with water. (*Up to dressing-table.*) I shall massage it gently with this delicious cream. Smell . . . (*She proffers a pot of cream.*)

GRACE (*sourly*). Very nice; I like Oatine better.

VIOLET. Well, Gladys Cooper uses this, and look at her skin!

GRACE (*unpinning her paper cap*). She married Arthur Bourchier, didn't she? (*Takes belt off.*)

VIOLET. No, you're thinking of Fay Compton.

GRACE. I'm very tired, you know; it was that last game we played, so energetic.

VIOLET (*crosses to chair L.*). Would you think it frightfully naughty of me if I smoke a cigarette?

GRACE. Not at all. (*Begins to undress.*)

VIOLET. I do so love a little puff before going to bye-byes.

GRACE (*takes off blouse, and then skirt. Sits on bed and takes off her shoes*). It's been a very successful evening, hasn't it?

VIOLET. Scrumptious.

GRACE. I do wish my daughter Amy had been here. She does make a party go so.

VIOLET. Fancy you having a grown-up daughter . . . (*Sits chair C.*) Just think now!

GRACE. Everybody says that. She's a bundle of talent, Amy!

VIOLET. I'm sure she is. Quite a bundle!

GRACE. She says the most killing things. Only the other day at tea a young man said to her, "A penny for your thoughts," and what do you think she said?

VIOLET (*taking her hair down*). I can't think. (*Crosses to L.*)

GRACE. She turned round quick as lightning and said, "They're worth more than that." (*She laughs immoderately.*)

VIOLET. Very quick, very quick indeed. (*Starts to undo dress.*)

GRACE. Whenever she goes out anywhere, she keeps the table in fits with her hospital stories. She was a V.A.D., you know, and really, the things she had to do to those poor soldiers, you'd die laughing.

VIOLET. I wonder if you would unhook me. (*Crosses to C.*)

GRACE. Certainly. (*She proceeds to do so.*)

VIOLET. One does feel so lost without a maid, doesn't one? Thank you so much. (*In execrable French . . . Pause.*) Oh! mon Dieu, com say frwor! (*Crosses R.*)

GRACE (*crosses up C. to washstand*). I beg your pardon?

VIOLET. I'm so sorry. When one's used to speaking French, one simply can't find the English words sometimes. (*She giggles affectedly.*)

GRACE (*going to washstand*). Amy's just the same; such a gift for languages. (*At washstand.*) No soap.

VIOLET. Pardon!

GRACE. There isn't any soap.

VIOLET. There's a small cake of Cuticura in my handkerchief drawer. (*She finds it; takes soap, gives to* GRACE.) Here you are; I never leave it out, servants are so untrustworthy nowadays.

GRACE. Oh! quite, quite. Thank you so much.

> (*While* GRACE *is washing rather noisily,* VIOLET *seizes the opportunity to put on her nightgown, which she does with becoming modesty, loosening all her underclothes first, then putting the nightgown over her head, and jumping until the cast-offs lie in a ring round her feet. She steps out of the ring with great refinement and proceeds to put her clothes away.*)

VIOLET. I must say this nightie was a bargain for $2/11\frac{3}{4}$. I always like Liberty's.

GRACE. I never allow them!

VIOLET. You probably did when you were my age. Talking of liberties . . . (*Crosses to chair L.*) What an outrageous man Mr. Harris is, isn't he?

GRACE (*drying herself*). I really never noticed.

VIOLET (*removing stockings*). My dear, the things he said to me when we were thinking of a charade. I didn't know where to look.

GRACE (*bitterly*). These mixed games always lead to unpleasantness. I remember when I was staying in the Cleveland Hydro at Swanage one Christmas . . .

VIOLET. Oh! I don't mind really, you know; travelling teaches one to look after oneself. I can pass anything off with a laugh.

GRACE (*crosses to front of bed*). I remember when I was staying at the Cleveland Hydro at Swanage one Christmas, there was a man . . .

VIOLET. It's so easy to manage men, you know, if only you have the knack, and being abroad so much, naturally one . . .

GRACE (*irately*). There was a man with a long red beard.

VIOLET (*greasing her face, crosses to table*). Oh! I can't stand a beard.

GRACE (*putting on her nightgown in the same way as* VIOLET). And if it hadn't been for Amy, I don't know what would have happened.

VIOLET. As I was saying, Mr. Harris . . . he pinched me very sharply, just at the beginning of the second syllable.

GRACE. How disgusting!

VIOLET. Naturally I ignored him for the rest of the evening, but it only shows you what men are.

GRACE. I always discourage that sort of thing; it's so common.

VIOLET. Sometimes one can't help oneself, but perhaps you don't find that?

GRACE. Any man will behave badly if he's led on.

VIOLET (*with slight rancour*). Really, I hope you're not insinuating.

GRACE. Certainly not; I was only stating a fact.

VIOLET. Well, with me, I'm afraid it's rather the reverse. The more I retire into my shell, the more the men come rushing after me.

GRACE. I promised Hubbard on his death-bed that I'd never look at another man, and I never have. (*Up at window.*)

VIOLET. Well, I must say one can do a lot without looking. (*She giggles.*)

GRACE. Really, Mrs. Banks; I don't consider that remark in the best of taste.

VIOLET. A little touch of the green-eyed monster, I'm afraid, Mrs. Hubbard.

GRACE. What was that you called me?

VIOLET. Please don't let us commence the New Year with a quarrel.

GRACE. I have no intention of quarrelling, but I must say I dislike lewdity.

VIOLET. What did you say?

GRACE (*crosses L.*). Lewdity; and if you can find a better word in French, you're at liberty to translate it.

VIOLET (*outraged*). Oh!

(*The rest of their toilet is concluded in an offended silence and* GRACE *wrestles unsuccessfully with the Venetian blind.*)

(*Grandly.*) Please, please allow me . . . I'm used to Venetians. We had them in our house at Boulogne when I was a girl. (*She tries to pull the string suddenly, and the whole blind falls down, almost crushing her beneath it.*)

GRACE. There now!

VIOLET. I am afraid you must have pulled the wrong string in the first place.

GRACE (*laughing hollowly, sits on bed L.*). That's very funny. Me pull the wrong string ! Very funny indeed. Oh, dear ; oh, dear !

VIOLET. Perhaps you would be so kind as to control your hysteria and assist me to draw the lace curtains.

GRACE. With pleasure.

(*They both unloop the lace curtains and drag them across.*)

VIOLET. I fear they will not meet.

GRACE. I could have told you that when I first saw them. I should think the watchword of this house is Economy. (*Crosses R. front of bed and lights candle.*)

VIOLET. On the contrary, Mrs. Rogers is the soul of generosity, besides being a personal friend of mine.

GRACE. I beg your pardon, I'm sure.

VIOLET. Granted. (*There is a silence, then she says with forced brightness.*) And so to bed. (*Crosses to bed L., lights her candle.*)

GRACE (*lighting her candle*). Will you turn out the gas, or shall I ?

VIOLET. I really don't mind ! (*She turns it out and gets into bed.*)

GRACE (*looking under her bed before getting into it*). I always do this in case of cat burglars.

VIOLET. How droll of you. I'm never nervous of that sort of thing.

GRACE. Indeed !

VIOLET. I expect it comes of being so cosmopolitan. Midnight visitors hold no terrors for me.

GRACE. I should be more inclined to conceal that fact than boast of it. Good night! (*She blows out her candle.*)

VIOLET. (*With great dignity.*) Good night! (*She blows out her candle and there is absolute silence and pitch darkness.*)

(*The clock strikes somewhere.*)

(*There is the sound of voices, the door opens, and* MR. HARRIS *and* MR. FRENCH *enter. They cannot be seen, but by their voices it is obvious that they are a trifle intoxicated. They close the door after them.*)

CHARLES (*enters door R.*). Got any matches? (*Feeling way along wall.*)

STEPHEN. Yes, half a mo'. (*He is heard fumbling.*)

CHARLES. This is our room all right, isn't it?

STEPHEN. Of course! I left them downstairs.

CHARLES. There'll be some on the bed-table. (*There is the sound of a lot of groping and fumbling.*)

STEPHEN. Can't you find any?

CHARLES. Hell! No!

STEPHEN. Well, I'm hanged if I'm going down those ruddy stairs again; it was bad enough coming up. We'll undress in the dark.

CHARLES. Oh! all right!

STEPHEN. That was a jolly good one you told about the woman in the bath. (*He laughs.*)

CHARLES (*also laughing*). A chap told it to me at the office last week.

STEPHEN. Do you know the one about the newly-married couple?

CHARLES. No.

STEPHEN. Well, there was a newly-married couple . . . stop me if you've heard it . . .

CHARLES. Righto.

STEPHEN. And they get to the hotel . . .

CHARLES. Oh! dash!

STEPHEN (*interrupting*). What's the matter now?

CHARLES. We've left our bags downstairs.

STEPHEN. Hell!

CHARLES. Go and get 'em, there's a pal.

STEPHEN. Not likely. I'm nearly undressed and stone cold.

CHARLES. So am I!

STEPHEN. I'll tell you. We'll go to bed in our shirts and have the bags up in the morning. (*Crosses to bed L.*)

CHARLES. All right!

STEPHEN. I'll take this bed. (*He approaches* VIOLET'S *bed.*)

(*She suddenly gives a piercing shriek.*)

VIOLET. If you come a step nearer, I'll scream the house down.

STEPHEN. Oh! my God!

(*There is the sound of a scuffle from* GRACE'S *bed; then she speaks in a very cooing and ingratiating voice.*)

GRACE. Well, young man, and what can I do for you?

CURTAIN

## CLASS

### 1924

### Introductory Speech before Scene I

Ladies and gentlemen: in the democratic England of to-day there is a good deal of discussion as to whether there are actual class differences or not. That all men are equal is undoubtedly a magnanimous theory, but strip the so-called "upper classes" of their luxurious surroundings, and the usual trappings of gilded ease, and, I ask you, what happens?

### Scene I

CHARACTERS:

Mrs. Higgins
Mr. Higgins
Alf Higgins
Ada (*his Wife*)
Maude

(*The Scene is an extremely squalid room in the East End. The table is laid for high tea. There are shrimps, winkles, etc., and a very sticky pot of jam. A canary in a minute cage in the window, and a few group photographs of* Alf's *wedding on the mantelpiece. When the curtain rises* Alf *is seated on a tilted-up chair with his feet on another, reading the " Star." He is in his shirt-sleeves, and has a cap on. He is smoking a Woodbine.* ADA, *in a pink blouse, with her hair in curlers, is laying the table.*)

ALF. What is Mother doing? We shall be frightfully late!

ADA. She always takes hours dressing.

ALF. I loathe getting in in the middle of the big picture.

ADA. Never mind, we can stay through the whole programme until it comes round again.

ALF (*scratching his head*). Look here, Ada, I'm a bit worried about Maude.

ADA. I don't think you need be. She's absolutely capable of looking after herself.

ALF. I'm not so sure. She's so liable to allow herself to be carried away by her emotions.

ADA. Hasn't she sent a telegram or anything?

ALF. No; she just went straight out of the house on Saturday without a word. I think Mother's getting anxious.

ADA. It's her own fault, really, dear. Let's face it. She was awfully tiresome over that fried fish.

ALF. Yes, but you know what she is. I've always realised that it's necessary to humour her over trifles.

(*Enter* MR. HIGGINS. *He is an oldish man with grey hair and a very old stained suit.*)

MR. H. This weather's ghastly. (*He hangs up his overcoat on a peg.*)

ADA. Perfectly fiendish.

MR. H. Isn't tea ready yet?

ALF. We're waiting for Mother, as usual.

ADA. Where have you been?

MR. H. Well, as a matter of fact I dropped into the "Green Man" and had a couple of Guinnesses with Joe Harris and some other fellows. Any news of Maude?

ALF. Not a thing.

MR. H. It's really extremely inconsiderate of her.

(*Enter* MRS. HIGGINS, *blousy and overdressed in third-rate flashy clothes.*)

MRS. H. My dears, I'm frightfully sorry, my hair's been driving me mad. Is the kettle boiling yet?

ADA. The tea's been made for hours, it will be black as ink.

MRS. H. Don't exaggerate, Ada darling. (*To* MR. H.) Cheer up, Bertie dear, we've got shrimps as it's your birthday.

MR. H. Oh! good!

MRS. H. You appear to be utterly plunged in impenetrable gloom.

ALF. Father's worried about Maude.

MRS. H. So are we all, but I've been trying not to think about it.

ADA. She'll be all right.

MRS. H. I feel dreadful about it. Where in heaven's name can she be?

ALF. She's probably gone down to the Bennetts.

MRS. H. No, I saw Mary Bennett yesterday; she hadn't heard from her either.

ADA. Oh well, we'd better have tea. Come along.

(*They all draw up their chairs and begin to have tea.*)

MR. H. (*helping himself to winkles*). Lend me a hair-pin, Emily dear.

MRS. H. You'd better have my brooch, it's much sharper. (*She unpins her brooch and hands it to him.*)

MRS. H. Thanks. I hope these are going to turn out better than the last lot you had.

(*He proceeds to pick out winkles, the door opens and* MAUDE *enters. She is flashily dressed, but she looks pale and rather furtive.*)

MRS. H. Maude! (*Kisses her absently.*)

MAUDE. Hullo, mother.

ALF. Where on earth have you been?

MAUDE. Don't be tiresome and brotherly, Alfred. I can't bear it. (*She kisses* MR. H.) Many happy returns of the day, Father. I've got a dreary little present for you. (*She gives him a small parcel.*)

MR. H. (*undoing it and disclosing a pair of coloured braces*). Thank you, Maude, you couldn't have given me anything I like better.

MAUDE (*taking off her hat and sitting down*). I'm glad you're pleased with them. I've been wracking my brains to think of something for you. Pass the shrimps, Ada.

ADA (*passing them*). Here you are, the salt's near you.

MRS. H. Where have you been, Maude?

ALF. Leave her alone, Mother, it's much wiser.

MAUDE. I've been away.

MRS. H. Yes, but where?

MAUDE. With the Bennetts.

MR. H. What?

MAUDE. You knew I was going.

MRS. H. Maude!

MAUDE (*impatiently*). Oh! what?

MRS. H. That is a deliberate lie.

MAUDE. Now look here, Mother . . .

MRS. H. I met Mary yesterday, she hadn't seen you for days.

MAUDE. How unfortunate. You shouldn't go out so much, Mother, it would save complications.

MR. H. Maude, what have you been doing?

MAUDE. For heaven's sake, Father, don't you start being tiresome too.

MRS. H. (*bursting into tears*). Oh, my God! Something terrible's happened. I know it, I can feel it in my bones.

ADA (*patting* MRS. H.'s *shoulder*). Don't, dear; don't give way.

MR. H. (*sternly*). Maude, tell us where you've been and put an end to this suspense.

MAUDE (*rising angrily*). Very well, I will. If you all persist in being so ridiculous and browbeating me. I determined to take a decisive step a long time ago, and now I've done it. I've been away with Harry Norfolk.

MR. H. What?

MRS. H. (*moaning*). Oh! Oh! Oh!

MAUDE. Don't go on like that, Mother. It's absurd. It's my life, and I fully intend to do what I like with it. I love Harry and he loves me, and we both love one another too much to marry. We neither of us feel that we could face the hideous little intimacies that constitute marriage. It kills all the romance and glamour, and ultimately love. How could it be otherwise? Particularly in these days of women's emancipation. When you and Mother married things were different; women were content to run houses and have babies and allow themselves to be lulled into a squalid domestic security. Nowadays women demand more. They demand passion and adventure and thrill. I'm in love for the first time in my life and I don't intend to sacrifice it for convention. I've done what I've done deliberately with my eyes open, and far from being ashamed, I'm positively elated. I mean to have complete freedom, physically and morally, and you can all exactly do what you choose about it.

### Introductory Speech before Scene II

You have witnessed an orthodox upper-class family in low-class surroundings dealing with the situation which might quite conceivably be common to both. We will now endeavour to present to you the reaction of the lower-class mind in higher-class surroundings in identically the same situation.

## Scene II

### CHARACTERS:

Sir Herbert Higgins, Bart.
Lady Higgins
Alfred Higgins
Lady Ada Higgins (*his Wife*)
Maude

(*The Scene is a beautifully furnished dining-room in Mayfair. Everything rich, luxurious and in exquisite taste. When the curtain rises* ALFRED (*in dinner-jacket*) *is reading the "Tatler" and smoking through a long onyx cigarette-holder.* ADA *is looking out of the window. She is wearing a beautifully simple dinner-dress and pearls. She is also smoking and sipping a cocktail. She turns and comes down and helps herself to an olive.*)

ALF. Where the 'ell's Ma? We shan't arf be late.

ADA. She always takes 'ours doing 'erself up.

ALF (*grumbling*). We'll get there bang in the middle of the six-reel drama.

ADA. Oh, shut up! we can sit the 'ole programme through 'til it comes round again, can't we?

ALF. I've got the wind up about Maudie.

ADA. Well, you needn't 'ave. Maudie's all right.

ALF. Oh, is she?

ADA. Ain't she sent a telegram or nothing?

ALF. No! She banged out of the 'ouse on Saturday.

ADA. It's all Ma's fault, she's such a "nagger." Look 'ow she went on over that grouse being a bit 'igh.

ALF. Oh, you know what she is; she wants a bit of getting round.

(*Enter* SIR HERBERT HIGGINS; *he is appropriately dressed in a dinner-jacket.*)

SIR H. Watcher, Alf, this weather's bleeding awful.

ADA. You've said it.

SIR H. Ain't dinner ready yet?

ALF. We're waiting for Ma; she's mucking about upstairs.

ADA. What you been up to?

SIR H. I been round to the Embassy and 'ad a couple of 'ow-d'yer-dos wiv Joe. Anyone seen our Maudie?

ALF. What a hope!

SIR H. Coo! Lummie! What a cow!

(*Enter* LADY H. *in an exquisite cloak, dress and fan.*)

LADY H. My 'air's been driving me fair batty. Why ain't the food up?

ADA. It ain't no use us ringing for it 'til you've finished fixing your face. (*She rings for it.*)

LADY H. Oh! look a bit brighter, Bert, for the love of Gawd! It's yer birthday, ain't it?

SIR H. Yus.

LADY H. Well then, Gloomy Gus.

ALF. Pa's worried about Maudie.

LADY H. So I should think; ungrateful little slut.

ADA. Oh, Maudie's O.K.

LADY H. I don't know where she's got to; she ain't with May Bennett 'cos I saw 'er yesterday.

(*Two* FOOTMEN *enter.*)

ADA. Oh well, let's 'ave a bite. Come on.

(*They all sit down.*)

(FOOTMEN *serve the soup and go out.*)

SIR H. This soup's blarsted 'ot.

LADY H. Oh! shut yer face.

(*The door opens and* MAUDIE *enters. She is attractively dressed in travelling clothes.*)

Maudie !

MAUDIE. What oh ! Mum. (*She kisses her.*)

ALF. Wat 'ave you been a-doing of ?

MAUDIE. Now look 'ere, Alf, you just keep your tongue between your teeth and leave me be. (*She kisses* SIR HERBERT.) 'Ere, Pa old cock, comps of the season and all that ; there's something to go on with. (*She gives him a small parcel.*)

SIR H. (*opening it and disclosing some wonderful links*). Blimey ! Look, Ma, ain't they bonza ?

MAUDIE. Oh well, as long as you're pleased. This 'at's giving me a 'eadache. (*She takes it off and sits down.*)

LADY H. Maudie, where 'ave you been ?

ALF. Oh, cheese it, Ma ; leave the poor girl alone.

MAUDIE. Where d'yer think I been ?

LADY H. 'Ow the devil do I know ?

MAUDIE. I been with May Bennett.

LADY H. You dirty little liar.

MAUDIE. Now look 'ere . . .

LADY H. I saw 'er yesterday at the Grosvenor 'Ouse Bazaar.

MAUDIE. You ought to stay in more, nosy parker.

SIR H. Wat's 'appened to you ?

MAUDIE. Nothing.

LADY H. You've gone wrong ; I can feel it in me bones. I'm like that. Not clairvoyant, but septic.

MAUDIE. Well, if you want it you shall 'ave it. I bin off with 'Arry.

SIR H. 'Arry. 'Arry Norfolk?

MAUDIE. Yus. Now then!

SIR H. You . . . you . . .

MAUDIE. Now you shut up, Pa. I know which side me bread's buttered.

LADY H. Oh, my Gawd!

MAUDIE. 'E loves me, and I love 'im, and we ain't the marrying sort neither. There ain't nothing in marriage nowadays, any'ow. Women know a damn sight too much; they've learnt 'ow to 'ave a bit of fun when they want it wiv'out tying theirselves up until Kingdom comes. I'm in love good and proper. You can lay your shirt on that. All right, all right. And I ain't goin' to do it in by muckin' about, see? Wat I've done I've done, and I'm proud of it, and if you don't like it you can all bloody well go to 'ell.

BLACK OUT

# CAT'S CRADLE

1928

CHARACTERS:

MISS LILIAN MAWDSLEY
MISS EVA TASSEL

*The Scene is the back view of two suburban villas. The two small gardens are separated by a low brick wall. At the back of each are French windows leading into the respective drawing-rooms—both gardens are very neat.*

(*When the curtain rises it is about* 8.30 *on a summer evening.* MISS MAWDSLEY *appears at her French windows carrying a saucer of milk—she is dressed rather austerely in a blouse and skirt—she wears pince-nez, and her hair is done rather high on her head.*)

MISS M. (*calling*). Minnie—Minnie—Min, Min, Min, Min, Min—come here, you bad cat. (*She puts the saucer of milk down on the step and retires indoors.*)

(MISS TASSEL *comes out of her house—she is elaborately dressed in a violet-coloured tea-gown—her hair is fair and shingled, she is wearing gauntlet gardening gloves and carries a cigarette in a long holder in one hand and a small green watering-can in the other. She looks cautiously over the wall into* Miss Mawdsley's *garden, and seeing no one there, proceeds to water her plants—humming a little tune as she does so.* Miss Mawdsley *reappears at the French windows and comes out into the garden.* Miss Tassel *sees her, but pretends not to, and continues to hum nonchalantly.*)

Miss M. Good evening, Miss Tassel.

Miss T. (*affectedly*). Oh dear—what a fright you gave me.

Miss M. I'm sure I'm very sorry.

Miss T. Oh, not at all. I've been terribly nervy ever since my last operation.

Miss M. It's a fine night.

Miss T. Quaite, quaite, perfect——

Miss M. We shall have a full moon.

Miss T. Lovely—too lovely. Whenever I see a full moon I *do* believe in fairies—don't you?

Miss M. Well, to be frank, Miss Tassel, I don't.

Miss T. Neither do I really—I just like pretending—I live in a world of my own, you know.

Miss M. I suppose you 'aven't seen my Minnie anywhere, 'ave you?

Miss T. Your what, Miss Mawdsley?

Miss M. My Minnie—my cat. I thought you might have noticed her in your world—she doesn't seem to be in mine.

Miss T. No—I fear—I haven't.

Miss M. She's mousing, sure as fate. Minnie—Min,

Min, Min, Min—I can't bear 'er to be out too late—you never know what might happen.

MISS T. Quaite.

MISS M. How are your nasturtiums?

MISS T. Quaite extraordinary—they grow so absurdly quickly. I feel just like Jack and the Beanstalk. (*She laughs affectedly.*)

MISS M. Something seems to have gone wrong with mine—look!

MISS T. (*craning over the wall*). My deah—how dreadful! What's that black thing?

MISS M. (*flicking it away*). Only a bootlace.

MISS T. I thought it was a great black worm.

MISS M. I can't 'elp feeling Minnie's been up to a bit of no good with my forget-me-nots—they were as right as rain yesterday, and look at 'em now.

MISS T. (*peering*). Are those forget-me-nots?

MISS M. What did you think they were, starfish?

MISS T. The light's so bad—it's difficult to see——

MISS M. I'm afraid Minnie's been rolling about on them—she dearly loves to play, you know.

MISS T. Such a pretty cat.

MISS M. Very nice markings and intelligent. Well, when I say she's human I'm underrating her.

MISS T. Fancy!

MISS M. Only the other day—you would 'ave laughed—oh dear, oh dear. (*She laughs.*)

MISS T. What happened?

MISS M. Well, you know that young couple from number fourteen? They popped in last Sunday evening quite unexpected. Well, it was Vera's evening out and I didn't know what to do, but you know you can't be inhospitable, so I said stay to supper if you don't mind taking pot luck—I knew there was some cold mutton over from Saturday and a half a blancmange and some prunes—so we all 'ad the mutton—Vera'd left the table laid before she went—and then I said, "Excuse me a moment," and down I went to the kitchen and there on the floor under the sink was a glass dish with only one prune in it—you could 'ave knocked me down with a feather—I looked under the table and there was Minnie washing herself. "Minnie," I said—"Minnie, you bad cat, what 'ave you done with them pruins?" She never looked up, so again I said very sternly, "Minnie, what 'ave you done with them pruins?" My dear, would you believe it, she gave me one look and walked straight out of the kitchen. I 'adn't the 'eart to scold her—she makes believe they're mice, you know!

MISS T. Charming; quaite, quaite charming. As a matter of fact, Miss Mawdsley, I have for a long time been wishing to discuss a certain subject with you.

MISS M. How d'you mean?

MISS T. Well, it's rather delicate. I hardly know where to begin.

MISS M. If you're alluding to our slight upset of last week, Miss Tassel, as I told you at the time it was nobody's fault. Vera took off the lid of the dustbin and whatever you found in your rockery must have blown there.

MISS T. Not at all—all that is forgiven and forgotten. This is something quite different—something much nearer my heart—it's about my Walter.

MISS M. What's 'e been up to?

MISS T. He hasn't been up to anything—that's just the trouble.

MISS M. In what way?

MISS T. Well, we're both women of the world, I trust.

MISS M. Yes—go on.

MISS T. It's wiser to speak frankly.

MISS M. By hall means.

MISS T. Well, Walter's getting a big cat now, and we feel, both my sister and I, that it's haigh time he—er—er—became—er—intimate with some other cat of his own station.

MISS M. Didn't you 'ave him arranged?

MISS T. No—I'm afraid not.

MISS M. You always ought to 'ave tom cats arranged, you know—it makes 'em so much more companionable.

MISS T. I never believe in tampering with nature.

MISS M. Well, what can I do for you?

MISS T. Well, I thought him and your Minnie, for instance.

MISS M. (*outraged*). My Minnie!

MISS T. Well, why not?

MISS M. I fear you don't understand, Minnie's not that kind of cat at all.

MISS T. How do you know?

MISS M. She's led a very sheltered life.

MISS T. But surely——

MISS M. I'm afraid I couldn't allow it.

MISS T. Aren't you being just the tayniest bit selfish?

MISS M. In what way?

MISS T. Well, you know life's life all the world over, and you can't escape from it. You're standing in the way of Minnie's happiness.

MISS M. Happiness!—Oh, Miss Tassel—— 'Ow can you? If I thought Minnie 'arboured such ideas after 'er life 'ere with me I'd never forgive meself.

MISS T. Facts are facts, you know. I've seen your Minnie walking up and down with ever such a wistful look in her eye.

MISS M. I don't know what to say—I don't really—I feel quite strange.

MISS T. (*grandly*). Of course in the circles I move in—the facts of life are discussed quaite quaite openly—— False modesty is so—er—middle class, don't you think?

MISS M. False modesty's one thing, Miss Tassel, and loose thinking's another.

MISS T. I beg your pardon.

MISS M. Granted as soon as asked.

MISS T. Are you insinuating——

MISS M. I'm insinuating nothing, Miss Tassel—but Minnie is not as other cats—as I said before, her life has been very secluded—I merely don't care to picture her in any—er—peculiar situation.

MISS T. Well, I only hope she won't lose her fur as she gets older.

MISS M. Lose 'er fur? What do you mean?

MISS T. If you had read as much as I have, Miss Mawdsley, you would realise that repression is a very bad thing.

MISS M. Minnie's as 'ealthy a cat as you'd meet in a day's march.

MISS T. At present perhaps—but if in your narrow-mindedness you refuse to allow her to fulfil her natural destiny——

MISS M. And what if I don't consider your Walter to be Minnie's natural destiny?

MISS T. That, Miss Mawdsley, is what the French would call un autre pair de souliers!

MISS M. I've no wish to quarrel with you, Miss Tassel, but I must say you've surprised me.

MISS T. (*laughing*). Surprised you! My poor Miss Mawdsley—surprised you—that's very funny.

MISS M. Funny I may be—but mark my words, all these modern discussions of everything only lead to immorality—you've only got to read the papers to see that.

MISS T. That's apparently all you do read, Miss Mawdsley.

MISS M. (*stiffly*). Good night.

(MISS MAWDSLEY *goes towards her house.*)

MISS T. Miss Mawdsley.

MISS M. (*turning*). Yes?

MISS T. I fear that perhaps we have both been a trifle hasty.

MISS M. That's true.

MISS T. If I said anything to offend you, I can only say I'm sorry.

MISS M. (*returning*). Well, of course, if you put it like that, I'm sure—I——

MISS T. I was wondering if you'd care for a cutting from my Dorothy Perkins——

MISS M. You're very kind.

MISS T. I'll send it over to-morrow.

MISS M. (*after a slight pause*). Where is your Walter now?

Miss T. He's indoors asleep.

Miss M. There's no doubt about it, 'e's a fine cat.

Miss T. It's very sweet of you to say so.

Miss M. I was comparing 'im in my mind the other day with that tabby of Mrs. Pedworth's.

Miss T. Mangy brute.

Miss M. Horrible cat—he's always coming sniffing round 'ere after Minnie—but fortunately she keeps 'erself to 'erself.

Miss T. Are you still definitely opposed to my little plan?

Miss M. Well, I don't quite know—you see——

Miss T. You don't think that if I let Walter out to-night—and if you—er—allowed Minnie to walk in the garden by herself, that, er, what with the moon and everything——

Miss M. Perhaps—it would be rather romantic in a sort of way.

Miss T. Then shall we consider that as settled.

Miss M. Yes.

Miss T. About ten o'clock.

Miss M. That's rather late.

(*Suddenly there is a dreadful caterwauling off stage left.* Miss Mawdsley *gives a cry and goes hurriedly off. She returns in a moment carrying* Minnie, *a large tabby cat, in her arms; she walks straight into the house.*)

(*Grimly over her shoulder.*) Too late!

Black Out

## RULES OF THREE

1928

### ANNOUNCEMENT

(ANNOUNCER *comes on from I.E.R. to Centre.*)

ANNOUNCER. Ladies and gentlemen, there has been a good deal of argument in the papers lately as to the general staleness of the English Drama. There have been bitter complaints to the effect that there *are no new* ideas any more. We now intend to demonstrate to you *our* point of view on the matter, which is that new ideas are not necessary, and that it is only the *treatment* that is important. We propose to show a perfectly commonplace situation as it would be handled by three celebrated dramatists. The situation is the Eternal Triangle. A wife is surprised during a scene with her lover by the unexpected entrance of her husband.

(*Moves to P.S.*)

First of all as Sir James Barrie would write it.

(*Exit I.E.L.*)

### 1. SIR JAMES BARRIE

CHARACTERS:

THE WIFE
THE HUSBAND
THE LOVER

(*The* WIFE *is darning socks by the fire.*)

WIFE (*pensively*). Ah me—I often wonder if all the little pink toes of all the little pink babies in the world were counted, how many there would be.

(*Enter L. the* LOVER.)

LOVER. Jeannie!

WIFE (*rising, comes D.R.C.*). Why have you come?

LOVER. I heard your voice in the wood.

WIFE. You couldna' have heard any such thing, James MacTagget, and it's a great fanciful fool you are.

LOVER. Jeannie!

WIFE. Whisht, man—away with you.

LOVER. I love you, Jeannie. I've loved you since ever I was a bairn no higher than a hiccough!

WIFE. Are you forgetting that I am a wife, James?

LOVER. Nay, I'm remembering it. The wife of a man who doesna' love or understand your ways.

WIFE. Ah, but you're wrong—John's well enough—my ways are not so difficult to grasp—I'm naught but a little shrivelled nut of a woman——

LOVER. You're a pixie to me.

WIFE. Thank you, James—a pixie's a chancy thing to be.

LOVER (*passionately*). I had a mind to be a great poet once, but the fairies made mock of me and I became an insurance agent.

WIFE. A great big brown insurance agent.

LOVER. Behind each of the company's policies I hear your laugh, and a winsome, cuddlesome sort of laugh it is. It seems to say, come away, James MacTagget, and learn how not to grow up. I'll teach you. I'll teach you.

WIFE. I *could* teach you that.

LOVER. Will you?

WIFE. Listen now—do you know how many babies there are in the world?

LOVER. No.

WIFE. Then multiply the answer by seven and you'll make a rainbow.

LOVER. Jeannie—come with me. (*He crushes her to him*).

WIFE. No, no!

LOVER. Don't send me to the workhouse of might have beens.

(*Enter the* HUSBAND *R.*)

HUSBAND. Jeannie!

WIFE. Oh!

HUSBAND. What does this mean?

WIFE (*laughing*). What a solemn face—sit down while I get your tea—you'd better be going, James.

HUSBAND. Tea—I'll not taste your tea.

WIFE. Go, James.

HUSBAND. Stay.

WIFE. Go—what fools men are——

HUSBAND. Stay!

WIFE. Verra well, stay—you great quarrelsome schoolboys. If I were the mother of either of you, I'd spank you and put you to bed—come, shake hands now.

LOVER. I'll not shake hands—I love Jeannie, John, and I'll make no bones about it. Good-bye.

(*He goes out L.*)

HUSBAND. Is this true?

WIFE. Yes.

HUSBAND. Why did you not go with him?

WIFE (*putting her head on* HUSBAND'S *shoulder*). Because it's you I love—you with your great laugh and your great hands and the tenderness in your eye when you see a baby having its bath and the gentleness in your voice when you take me in your arms and call me Mrs. Woodlesome Whatnot.

HUSBAND (*taking her in his arms*). Mrs. Woodlesome Whatnot!

BLACK OUT.
CLOSE TABS.

(ANNOUNCER *comes on I.E.L.*)

ANNOUNCER. And now as Frederick Lonsdale would treat it.

(*Exit I.E.L.*)

2. FREDERICK LONSDALE

(*The* WIFE *is discovered dancing to a gramophone.*)

(*The* LOVER *enters L.*)

LOVER. Duchesses don't dance as well as they used to.

WIFE. No, my dear, but much more.

LOVER. Where's Johnnie?

WIFE (*stopping the gramophone*). Still in the House of Lords, I think.

LOVER. My God, Jean, you look chic.

WIFE. It isn't difficult to look chic nowadays. One only needs line and lipstick.

LOVER. I saw the Duke of Belgravia at lunch.

WIFE. I thought he was dead.

LOVER. He is, but he won't lie down.

WIFE. Do you think it was quite decent of you to come here?

LOVER. Decency be damned! I love you.

WIFE. As a man loves a woman or as a gentleman loves a gentlewoman?

LOVER. All four.

(*The* BUTLER *enters with cocktails R.*)

WIFE. I've got a new cocktail for you.

LOVER. What's it called?

WIFE. The Debrett Dollop!

LOVER. Do you like being a butler, Finsbury?

BUTLER. Very much, your Grace. We are the only class left with any manners.

LOVER. What about the Upper Ten?

BUTLER. They only have bedside manners.

(*He goes out R.*)

WIFE. I don't know what the lower orders are coming to.

LOVER. You're a silly woman, Jean, with the brains of a louse.

WIFE. Dear James, you're drunk—you must have been lunching with your mother.

LOVER. Nevertheless, I love you.

WIFE (*surrendering herself to him*). Kiss me like you did last Wednesday in the Royal Enclosure at Ascot.

(*He kisses her violently.*)

(*The* HUSBAND *enters R.*)

HUSBAND. My dear Jean—you might have left the door open.

LOVER (*looking up*). Hullo, Johnnie.

HUSBAND. By God, Jimmie, you're an awful swine—is there any cocktail?

WIFE. Not a drain. I love Jimmie, you know.

HUSBAND. Of course I know—everybody knows. It makes a damned good story—I've been dining out on it for weeks.

LOVER. What shall we do about it?

HUSBAND. What is there to do—I can't divorce her because I have to have a mistress for my father's old place.

WIFE. Don't discuss me so cold-bloodedly—I'm not an electric hare.

LOVER. Well, we'd better go on as we are, I suppose.

HUSBAND. All right. (*Crosses to C.*) Here's an extra latchkey.

LOVER. Thanks—cheerio!

(*Exit L.*)

HUSBAND. Nice fellow.

WIFE. Johnnie, I'm awfully fond of you.

HUSBAND. Why?

WIFE. Because you're a very great gentleman.

HUSBAND. What is a very great gentleman?

WIFE. I don't know. I go to so few theatres.

BLACK OUT.
CLOSE TABS.

## RULES OF THREE

(*French Farce*)

CHARACTERS:

JEANNE
JACQUES
JEAN
ANNETTE

(*The Scene is* JEANNE'S *bedroom. This whole episode must be played at lightning speed.*

(*The telephone rings.*)

(ANNETTE *runs on.*)

ANNETTE (*at telephone*). 'Allo—yes, m'sieu—no, m'sieu—yes, m'sieu—no, m'sieu—certainly, m'sieu——

(*She rushes off.*)

(JEANNE *rushes on in highly-coloured pyjamas.*)

JEANNE (*at telephone*). Jacques—darling—yes, angel. No, angel—quickly, quickly—— (*Makes kissing noise.*) Yes, yes—darling, darling—— (*She hangs up telephone.*) Annette—Anette——

(ANNETTE *rushes in.*)

ANNETTE. Yes, madame.

JEANNE. My peignoir, quickly.

ANNETTE. Yes, madame.

(*She rushes off.*)

(JEANNE *goes to telephone.*)

JEANNE (*at telephone*). Elysee 9468—yes, yes—no no—— Hallo—— Gaston—is it you?—— Yes—— No, I don't think so—very well—hurry—— (*She puts telephone down.*)

(ANNETTE *rushes in—a bell rings.*)

Quickly, Annette—quickly—it is he—answer the door. (*She puts on her peignoir.*)

(ANNETTE *rushes off.*)

(JACQUES *rushes on.* JEANNE *flies into his arms. They kiss passionately.*)

JACQUES (*between kisses*). Darling—beloved—angel—precious—saint—divinity——

(ANNETTE *rushes on with a pair of pyjamas.*)

ANNETTE. Here, m'sieu.

(JACQUES *rushes off.*)

JEANNE. You can go now, Annette.

ANNETTE. Yes, madame.

(*There is the sound of the front door slamming.*)

JEANNE. My God, my husband !

(JEAN *rushes on.*)

JEAN (*clasping her in his arms*). My darling wife—I have returned from Lyons three days earlier than I expected——

JEANNE. Jean, Jean—how glad I am—— (*She casts an anxious look at the door.*)

JEAN. You seem worried, my angel.

JEANNE. It is the heat—will you go and close the spare room window.

JEAN. Certainly, beloved.

(*He rushes off L.*)

(JACQUES *rushes on R. in pyjamas.*)

JACQUES (*clasping her in his arms*). My enchantress——

JEANNE (*pushing him back*). Hide quickly, quickly——

JACQUES. Very well——

(*He rushes off R.*)

(JEAN *rushes on L.*)

JEAN. There is no window in the spare room.

JEANNE. My foolish darling—it was a joke—— Run and fetch my handbag for me, it is on the piano.

JEAN. Imperious angel.

(*He rushes towards R.*)

JEANNE. No, no—on the piano.

JEAN. How stupid—I'd forgotten the piano was in the bathroom.

(*He rushes off L.*)

(JACQUES *rushes on R.*)

JACQUES (*taking her in his arms*). Wonderful—wonderful—wonderful——

JEANNE. Quick, quick, my husband——

(JACQUES *leaps into bed.*)

(JEAN *rushes on with a pair of shoes.*)

JEAN. Here are your shoes. They were in the bureau.

JEANNE. My darling.

(JEAN *sees* JACQUES' *hat.*)

JEAN (*furiously*). What is this?

JEANNE. It is your mother's. She came here this afternoon.

JEAN. Where is she?

JEANNE (*hysterically*). In there! (*She points R. and—* JEAN *rushes off.*)

(JEANNE *jumps into bed with* JACQUES. ANNETTE *rushes on in pyjamas, looks round and then beckons.*)

(JEAN *rushes on.*)

ANNETTE. It's all right—the coast's clear.

JEAN (*clasping her in his arms*). My darling!

BLACK OUT

# THE LIDO BEACH

1928

## CHARACTERS :

The Contessa
Lady Fenchurch
Sir Charles Fenchurch
Young Man
Baroness Kurdle
Mr. Clark
Lady Millicent
Lady Saltwood
Lady Verlap
Violet
Jane
Baby
Grace

### Opening

(*The Scene is the Lido Beach. There should be a back-cloth with Excelsior Hotel on it up against bright blue sky. In the foreground a row of cabanas with coloured striped awnings and coloured mattresses and cushions.*)

(*When the curtain rises the* Chorus *is discovered in a straight line across the stage, with their hands on their knees looking out front. Some are in bathing dresses and some in gaily coloured pyjamas. There is a general air of sunshine and colour and gaiety.*)

## Opening Chorus

All.

A narrow strip of sand,
Where Byron used to ride about,
While stately ships would glide about
The sea on either hand.
But now the times have changed,
For civilised society
With infinite variety
Has had it rearranged.
No more the moon
On the still Lagoon
Can please the young enchanted,
They must have this,
And they must have that,
And they take it all for granted.
They hitch their star
To a cocktail bar,
Which is all they really wanted.
That narrow strip of sand
Now reeks with assininity.
Within the near vicinity
A syncopated band
That plays the Blues—all the day long—
And all the old Venetians say
They'd like a nice torpedo
To blow the Lido away.

(Chorus *go up stage and form several groups.*)

(*Two* Wives *enter top E.R. and two top E.L. and come down to footlights.*)

WIVES.

Beneath the blue skies
Of Sunny Italy
We lie on the sand.
But please understand
We're terribly grand.
We firmly married
The old nobility,
But we can spend happy days here,
Take off our stays here,
Tarnish our laurels,
Loosen our morals.
Oh ! you'll never know
The great relief it is
To let our feelings go.
We're comme il faut
You see, and so
It doesn't matter what vulgarity
We show !

(*Two* HUSBANDS *enter top R. and two top L. and come down and take up positions on L. of each* WIFE.)

HUSBANDS.

Ladies of abundant means
And less abundant minds,
Although we're not romantic
We crossed the cold Atlantic
To choose a few commercial queens
Of different sorts and kinds.
Returning with a cargo
Of girlhood from Chicago,
Tho' we regret it more from day to day,
We think it only fair to you to say :

It wasn't for your beauty that we married you,
It wasn't for your culture or your wit,
It wasn't for the quality that Mrs. Glyn describes
As " It," just it.
It wasn't your position in Society
That led us on to making such a fuss——

(*Four* WIVES *start going off L., four* HUSBANDS *start going off R., singing the last three lines.*)

Forgive us being frank,
But your balance in the bank
Made you just the only wives for us.

(*At exit of* HUSBANDS *and* WIVES, CHORUS *form a straight line across stage and sing this verse :*)

ALL.

This narrow strip of sand
Makes something seem to burst in us,
Brings out the very worst in us ;
But kindly understand,
We've got the blues all the day long
And every year we always say
We'd like a nice torpedo
To blow the Lido away !

(*Half exeunt R., half L.*)

(*At the end of the Opening Chorus there is a general buzz of conversation. Four people playing Bridge outside a cabana on the L. are quarrelling furiously.* LADY M. *is lying on mattress, R.*)

CONTESSA. What did you play that for ?

SIR C. Because it seemed to me the most suitable card to play.

CONTESSA. I've always thought you a dreary old fool, Charles!

LADY F. Darling Contessa—don't be so tiresome.

CONTESSA. We're playing Bridge—not animal grab.

(*A* YOUNG MAN *in a bathing suit approaches the table,* 1 *E.L.*)

YOUNG MAN. Are we lunching upstairs dressed or down here undressed?

CONTESSA. Mind your own business!

YOUNG MAN. It is my business. I'm paying for lunch.

LADY F. Upstairs then, dear—it's more expensive.

YOUNG MAN. Look—here comes a photographer.

(EVERYBODY *at once screams and rushes eagerly off the stage.* SIR CHARLES *stops and looks at cards and then rushes off. After a moment they return, smiling with satisfaction. The* YOUNG MAN *lies down at bottom of mattress, R.*)

SIR C. Well, I double.

(*The* BARONESS KURDLE, *an elderly woman, comes out of her cabana in a dressing-gown—she is large and extremely feminine. She is followed by* MR. CLARK *from top E.L.*)

LADY M. Who's this? I'm new to the Lido.

CONTESSA. That's the Baroness Kurdle. Just an Austrian girl.

BARONESS. Where iss my oil?

LADY M. Your what, dear?

BARONESS. Oil—somebody have pinched him.

MR. CLARK. Pinched who?

BARONESS. My oil. It iss my hour for sunburn.

LADY M. (*holding up bottle*). Is this it?

(MR. CLARK *pulls mattress down stage.*)

BARONESS. Ach yes—Mr. Clark, you will please rub my back—I my front can do myself——

LADY M. I never know, Baroness, why you go to all this trouble, anyhow.

BARONESS (*taking off her dressing-gown and displaying a slightly inadequate bathing costume*). Sunburn is very becoming—but only when it is even—one must be careful not to look like a mixed grill. (*She undoes the shoulder-straps of her bathing suit and lies face downwards on a mattress.*) Mr. Clark, you will please begin.

(MR. CLARK *dutifully begins to rub her back with oil.*)

LADY M. Look—there's a photographer.

BARONESS. My wrap—my God! my wrap—my God!

(EVERYBODY *at once rushes off all entrances L. The* BARONESS *is the last one off the stage.*)

(VIOLET, JANE, BABY *and* GRACE *enter top E.R. They are all exquisitely dressed.*)

VIOLET. What's that crowd over there?

JANE. Only a camera-man.

BABY. Really, the way these people rush after publicity is disgusting—we don't go on like that.

GRACE. They're amateurs, dear—and we're professionals.

(*They come down stage to footlights.*)

QUARTETTE: "*Little Women*"
VIOLET, JANE, BABY and GRACE

I
(*Bus: as arranged.*)

ALL.

We're little girls of certain ages
Fresh from London Town,
Like an instalment plan of Drage's
We want so much down.
We have discovered years ago
That flesh is often clay,
We're not a new sin,
We're on the loose in
Quite the nicest way.
We have renounced domestic cares
For ever and for aye.
We're not so vicious,
Merely ambitious.
If there must be love,
Let it be free love.

*Refrain*

We're little women,
Alluring little women,
Cute but cold fish,
Just like goldfish
Looking for a bowl to swim in.
We lead ornamental
But uncreative lives,
We may be little women,
But we're not good wives.

VIOLET.

I am just an ingenue
And shall be till I'm eighty-two ;
At any rude remark my spirit winces,
I've a keen religious sense,
But in girlish self-defence
I always have to put my faith in princes.

ALL.

Do not trust them, gentle maiden,
They will kick you in the pants !

RUTH.

I'm not a type that is frequently seen,
I wear my hair in a narrow bang ;
I have remained at the age of eighteen
Since I left home in a charabanc.
Tho' men all pursue me
When they woo me
They construe me as innocent ;
But when I hear things suggestively phrased
I'm not unduly amazed.

ALL.

It takes far more than that to wake
Sweet wonder in her eyes !

JANE.

I waste no time on things
That other girls are arch about,
I much prefer to march about alone.
I am a baby vamp,
I'd take a postage stamp,
I just believe in grabbing
Anything that's offered me.

If Mother Hubbard proferred me—a bone
I should not be upset,
Have the darned thing re-set.

ALL.

Much further than the Swannee River
She keeps her old folks at home !

IVY.

I am a girl whose soul with domesticity abounds.
I know a man of six-foot-three who's worth a million pounds. (*Whoops.*)
Tho' he is like a brother
I haven't told my mother
He's given me a lovely house and grounds !

ALL.

Be it ever so humbug
There's no place like home.

*2nd Refrain*

ALL.

We're little women,
Alluring little women,
Cute but cold fish,
Just like goldfish
Looking for a bowl to swim in.
Tho' we're very clinging
Our independence thrives.
We may be little women
But we're not good wives.

(*They all exeunt* 1 *E.L. on the last four bars.*)

## THE ENGLISH LIDO

1928

CHARACTERS:

MR. FREEMAN
MRS. FREEMAN
ALICE
FRANKIE
OFFICIAL
MR. HARRIS
MRS. HARRIS
PHYLLIS
VI
GEORGIE
MRS. CLARK
MRS. JONES
MADGE
DORIS
DAISY KIPSHAW
HOCKEY PLAYERS, CHILDREN, CAMERA-MEN, BATHERS, ETC.

PRELIMINARY SPEECH

(ANNOUNCER *comes on in front of Tabs.*)

ANNOUNCER. Ladies and gentlemen, it has been suggested in several newspapers of late that English seaside resorts hold out fewer attractions to visitors than Continental ones. Any true patriotic Englishman naturally resents this reflection on our national gaiety, and Mr. Cochran perhaps more keenly than anyone—so he has determined to prove conclusively once and for all that no holiday resort in the world can equal in charm, gaiety and light-hearted care-free enjoyment an average watering-place on the shores of the English Channel.

### Opening Chorus

(*All the* Chorus *are discovered in a straight line across the stage.* Mr. *and* Mrs. Harris *in middle of line,* Mr. *and* Mrs. Freeman *to the L. of them.*)

All.

Hooray, hooray, hooray !
The holidays !
The jolly days,
When laughter, fun and folly days
Appear.
Hooray, hooray, hooray !
The laity
With gaiety
And charming spontaneity
Must cheer.

Mr. Harris.

I've left my bowler hat and rubber collar far behind.

Mrs. Harris.

I wish to God you'd left that awful Panama behind,
It looks gaga behind !

All.

But never mind, because the holidays are here,
Our tastes are very far from Oriental,

We have a very fixed idea of fun.
The thought of anything experimental
Or Continental
We shun.
We take to innovations very badly,
We'd rather be uncomfortable than not.
In fighting any new suggestion madly
We'd gladly
Be shot!
We much prefer to take our pleasures sadly
Because we're really quite contented with our lot.

(*The Scene is structurally the same as the Lido Scene, except that in place of cabanas there are bathing machines. The sky is leaden grey and there is a violent wind blowing. Some of the characters wear ill-fitting bathing costumes with Burberrys and mackintoshes over them, others are dressed respectively in flannels and blazers and plus-fours and cloth coats and skirts and very rumpled summer dresses. There broods over everything that air of complacent dreariness which is inseparable from any English seaside resort.*)

(*When the Opening Chorus is over, a very well-developed* WOMAN *of about thirty runs in from* 1 *E.R. to C.*)

WOMAN. I say, girls, what about a game of beach hockey?

1ST GIRL. Topping!

2ND GIRL. Righto!

3RD GIRL. Good egg!

(*About nine of them go off—leaving the stage empty except for the* HARRIS FAMILY *on the R. They sit in the two end chairs. And the* FREEMAN FAMILY *on the L., and a few odd* PEOPLE *strolling about.* MRS. FREEMAN *is vainly trying to put up a deck chair R. of bathing machine. Finally she sits down. An* OLD MAN *climbs up steps of bathing machine and looks through hole in the door.* MR. FREEMAN *sits down R. of bathing machine with a newspaper.*)

MR. F. 'I—come on out of it, nosie!

(OLD MAN *goes top E.R.*)

MRS. F. (*sits down*). That's the first time I've been 'ot for ten days. (*Is knitting.*)

MR. F. What are you grumblin' about?

MRS. F. I'm not grumblin', but it's my belief this place isn't as bracing as they said it was. I feel awful.

MR. F. (*wearily*). Oh, what's the matter with you?

MRS. F. Well, I'll tell you—I've got a cold, wind under the 'eart, I feel sick, and me feet hurt!

MR. F. What d'you think you are—a medical magazine?

MRS. F. Well, if you 'adn't 'ad hiccough all night I might 'ave got a bit of sleep and felt better!

MR. F. Where's Alice?

MRS. F. 'Elping Frankie on with his bathing things—'e loves the water.

(*Shrill screams of rage come from inside bathing machine.*)

MR. F. Yes, it sounds like it, don't it?

(ALICE, *a girl of about sixteen, in a very voluminous bathing gown, comes out of the bathing machine leading* FRANKIE, *a little boy of ten, clad only in striped bathing drawers—he is yelling loudly. Cross to R.*)

Can't you keep the child quiet?—yer ma's not feeling well.

ALICE. 'E found a beetle in 'is bucket.

(MR. FREEMAN *goes over to* FRANKIE.)

MR. F. 'Ere, 'ere, 'ere, Frankie, stop it—you're getting a big boy now—making all that fuss about a poor innocent beetle.

MRS. F. That child's been a bundle of nerves ever since we took him to see *Chang*.

(AN OFFICIAL *in uniform walks on and taps* MR. FREEMAN *on the shoulder*.)

OFFICIAL. Excuse me, this little lad must have a top to 'is bathing dress.

MR. F. Why—what for?

OFFICIAL. Corporation's rules.

(MRS. F. *gets up from chair and comes down stage.*)

MRS. F. Lot of nonsense—the child's under age.

OFFICIAL. Can't 'elp that, madam.

ALICE. 'E 'asn't got a top.

OFFICIAL. The Corporation's very strict about indecent exposure.

MR. F. Well, it's coming to something if a child of ten can't enjoy a state of nature without giving a lot of old ladies ideas.

OFFICIAL. England don't 'old with states of nature.

MRS. F. 'Ere—'e'd better 'ave my crochet sports jacket. (*Cross to R. She gives it to* ALICE, *who drapes it round* FRANKIE.) Will that do?

OFFICIAL. Yes—sorry to 'ave troubled you.

(*He goes off 2 E.L.*)

MR. F. Well, I'm damned!
ALICE. Come on, Frankie.

(*Takes him off 1 E.R.*)

MR. F. That boy looks effeminate. You going to have a bathe this morning?
MRS. F. Not unless you want me to die this afternoon.
MR. F. I'm off to 'ave a paddle. (*Cross to R.*)
MRS. F. Mind you take plenty of soda with it!

(MR. FREEMAN *is going off and collides with* MADGE *and* DORIS *on the way. They are crossing from R. to L.*)

MR. F. Pardon.
DORIS. Granted.

(SHE *and* MADGE *stroll across.*)

MADGE. Where was I?
DORIS. He was just holding your hand and the band was playing "The Mikado."
MADGE. Oh, yes—well, dear—I said "Keep your hands to yourself," and he said, "Why?" and I said, "You know why," and he said, "Come off it, Miss High and Mighty," and I said, "Don't be saucy," and he bought me some nougat and I didn't get home till two in the morning.

(*They go off.*)

MRS. H. (*reading the paper*). Fred!
HARRIS (*who has been sleeping*). 'Allo!
MRS. H. That murderer's been caught.

HARRIS. Which one?

MRS. H. Last Tuesday's.

HARRIS. Oh!

MRS. H. You can go and see the 'ouse where it 'appened. It's quite near 'ere. Mabel went yesterday and said it was lovely—blood all over everything.

HARRIS. Coo! We might take the children this afternoon.

MRS. H. All right. I'll cut some sandwiches.

(*Two* CHILDREN—GEORGIE *and* VI—*come running in screaming from* 1 *E.R. They go to their mother.*)

HARRIS. What's up now?

VI. Georgie hit me with his iron spade.

GEORGIE. No, I never!

VI. Yes, he did!

GEORGIE. No, I never!

MRS. H. Come 'ere, Georgie—that's the third time you've 'it Vi in two days—I'll teach you!

(*She bends him across her knee and smacks him—the noise is deafening.*)

HARRIS. Can't you leave the blighter alone?

MRS. H. Don't you tell me 'ow to bring up me own children!

HARRIS. The poor little bloke didn't mean it.

VI. Yes, 'e did.

HARRIS. You shut up. . . . (*He slaps her. She sets up a terrible howl.*)

VI (*screaming*). Ow! ow! ow! Father 'it me!

MRS. H. You great brute, you! (*Getting up and taking* VI *in her arms.*)

HARRIS. Brute, am I?

MRS. H. Be quiet, Vi—stop that noise!

HARRIS. I can't stand this—I'm going to get drunk——

(*Goes off top E.L.*)

MRS. H. That'll be a change——

(*A harassed mother*—MRS. CLARK—*enters pushing a screaming child in front of her. They get to C.*)

MRS. C. I brought you 'ere to enjoy yourself, and enjoy yourself you're going to! Now go on—paddle!

(*She smacks her hard and—the* CHILD *goes off screaming.* GEORGIE *and* VI *follow* 1 *E.R.*)

(MRS. CLARK *sits down exhausted next to* MRS. FREEMAN *R.*)

I'll never come to this place again as long as I live.

MRS. F. I don't think I shall live long enough to be able to!

(MRS. HARRIS *is fanning herself with her paper.*)

(MRS. JONES, *a weary-looking woman, comes on top E.R. and sits down next to her.*)

MRS. J. Good morning, Mrs. Harris.

MRS. H. Good morning.

MRS. J. I've just come from the 'ospital. My little Albert fell off a rock yesterday and cut 'is 'ead open——

(*They* ALL *come down stage.*)

"*Mother's Complaint*"

ALL.

We're all of us mothers,
We're all of us wives,
The whole depressing crowd of us.

With our kind assistance
The Motherland thrives.
We hope the nation's proud of us,
For one dreary fortnight
In each dreary year
We bring our obstreperous families here.
We paddle and bathe while it hails and it rains,
In spite of anæmia and varicose veins,
Hey nonny, ho nonny, no, no, no.
Our lodgings are frowsy,
Expensive and damp,
The food is indigestible.
We sit on the beach
Till we're tortured with cramp
And life is quite detestable.
The children go out with a bucket and spade
And injure themselves on the asphalt parade.
There's sand in the porridge and sand in the bed,
And if this is pleasure, we'd rather be dead.
Hey nonny, ho nonny, no, no, no!

(VI, PHYLLIS *and* GEORGE *rush on from* I *E.R.*)

VI. Mum, mum, Cissie Parker's seen a whale!

MRS. H. Don't you tell such lies, Violet Harris.

PHYLLIS. It's true, it's true—I saw it too—look there!

(ALICE *and* FRANKIE FREEMAN *rush on.*)

ALICE. Mother—mother—a great big whale!

MRS. F. May God forgive you, you wicked little fibber!

(*Several other* CHILDREN *rush on screaming, and all the* CHORUS—"*A whale, a whale!*" *Also*

GROWN-UPS. *Finally the* OFFICIAL *re-enters top E.L. and comes to C. of stage.*)

OFFICIAL. 'Ere, 'ere, 'ere—what's all this noise?

MRS. H. There's a whale—my Vi's seen a whale. Look, there it is!

(*Lots more* PEOPLE *rush on; the* OFFICIAL *produces some glasses and looks through them.*)

OFFICIAL. That's not a whale—that's Daisy Kipshaw, the Channel swimmer. She gets 'ere regularly every Friday morning from Boulogne.

(EVERYBODY *cheers.*)

(*Three* MEN *come on with cameras, and finally* DAISY KIPSHAW—*a very large woman in a bathing suit—comes on from* 1 *E.L. The three* MEN *with cameras take photos of her—one as she turns to pick up her cloak which she has dropped on getting to C. of stage. As she enters all the* CHORUS *take up lines across stage on O.P. side.*)

FINALE AND NUMBER FOR DAISY KIPSHAW

(*She comes C.*)

CHORUS.

Hail, Neptune's daughter,
The pride of Finsbury Park,
Behold a modest clerk
Is goddess of the water.
Hail, pioneer girl,
Tho' rain and wind have come,
You've swum and swum and swum,
You really are a dear girl

DAISY.

Kind friends, I thank you one and all
For your delightful greetings.
I merely heard my country's call
At patriotic meetings.

CHORUS.

Just think of that,
Just think of that,
She got her inspiration at
A patriotic meeting.
Oh, tell us more,
Oh, tell us more,
Oh, tell us what you do it for,
It must be overheating.

DAISY.

Kind friends, I thank you all again
And since you ask me to,
I will explain.

SONG : " *Britannia Rules the Waves* "

DAISY.

Like other chaste stenographers
I simply hate photographers,
I also hate publicity.

CHORUS.

She lives for sheer simplicity !

DAISY.

For any woman more or less
A photo in the daily press
Is horribly embarrassing.

CHORUS.

It must be dreadfully harassing.

DAISY.

The British male
May often fail,
Our faith in sport is shaken,
So English girls awaken
And save the nation's bacon!

*Refrain* I

(*Sung by* DAISY *alone first.*)

Up, girls, and at 'em,
And play the game to win.
The men must all give in
Before the feminine.
Bowl 'em and bat 'em
And put them on the run,
Defeat them every one,
Old Caspar's work is done.
We'll do our bit till our muscles crack,
We'll put a frill on the Union Jack.
If Russia has planned
To conquer us and
America misbehaves,
Up, girls, and at 'em,
Britannia rules the waves!

(*Bus. with* CHORUS *as arranged.*)

*Refrain* 2

DAISY AND CHORUS.

Up, girls, and at 'em,

And play the game to win.
The men must all give in
Before the feminine.
Bowl 'em and bat 'em,
And put them on the run,
Defeat them every one,
Old Caspar's work is done.

DAISY.
We'll do our bit till our muscles crack.

CHORUS.
We'll put a frill on the Union Jack.

DAISY.
If Russia has planned to conquer us and
America misbehaves,
Up, girls, and at 'em,
Britannia rules the waves.

*Refrain 3*

(*Spoken.*)
Up, girls, and at 'em,
Go out and win your spurs,
For England much prefers
Applauding amateurs.
Man is an atom,
So break your silly necks
In order to annex
Supremacy of sex.
Valiantly over the world we'll roam,
Husbands must wait till the cows come home.
The men of to-day
Who get in our way
Are digging their early graves.

Up, girls, and at 'em,
 Britannia rules the waves.

*Refrain 4*

DAISY AND CHORUS.
Up, girls, and at 'em,
 And play the game to win.
 The men must all give in
 Before the feminine.
Bowl 'em and bat 'em
 And put them on the run,
 Defeat them every one,
 Old Caspar's work is done.
We'll do our bit till our muscles crack,
We'll put a frill on the Union Jack.

DAISY.
Here's to the maid
Who isn't afraid,
 Who shingles and shoots and shaves.

CHORUS.
Up, girls, and at 'em !
 Britannia rules the waves !

(*Bus. of* CHORUS BOYS *getting in her way. They lift her up. As they* ALL *drop on stage*—

BLACK OUT)

# IGNORANCE IS BLISS

1928

## Scene I

SCENE: *The scene is a hotel bedroom of the 'nineties.*

(*A* YOUNG HUSBAND *and* WIFE *are ushered in by a very fat* PROPRIETRESS—*a chambermaid comes in after them with their luggage. The furniture is ugly and heavy, and on the R. is a large double brass bed.*)

PROPRIETRESS. Put the things down over there, Annie.

(ANNIE *puts bags at the end of sofa.*)

Come this way, please.

(*They come on and cross to front of sofa.*)

I think you'll be very comfy here. (*Shakes up bed.*)

HUSBAND. Thank you.

WIFE (*with an effort*). I'm sure we shall.

PROPRIETRESS. Married to-day?

HUSBAND } (*together*). { Oh no!
WIFE } { Oh yes!

PROPRIETRESS (*rubbing her hands*). Now, now, now, now! You mustn't be shy. (*To the* MAID.) Don't stand there gaping, Annie—run away.

ANNIE. Yes'm.

(*She crosses back of sofa and exits door C.*)

PROPRIETRESS. Do you know Worthing well?

(*Crosses to window O.P. side.*)

HUSBAND. No.

PROPRIETRESS. You can get a lovely view of the sea from this window 'ere—*h*ere.

WIFE (*gulping*). How nice.

PROPRIETRESS (*archly*). But I don't suppose you'll be looking out of the window much, will you? (*Crosses to centre.*)

WIFE. Oh, Harry!

HUSBAND. That will be all now, thank you, Mrs. Blake.

PROPRIETRESS (*crosses up to door, C*). If you want anything you've only got to ring for it, you know.

HUSBAND. Thanks—thanks very much.

PROPRIETRESS. Not at all—a pleasure—I like to see young things standing on the threshold of life, as it were.

(*She stands and looks at them, smiling. There is a long pause.*)

(HUSBAND *crosses to* WIFE *and takes off coat.*)

HUSBAND. Quite.

PROPRIETRESS (*conversationally, coming down stage*). I was born 'ere, you know, born and married and widowed all in Worthing.

WIFE (*nervously*). How nice.

PROPRIETRESS. It's the close season now—but it's very gay in the summer.

HUSBAND. It must be. (*Puts coat down on sofa.*)

PROPRIETRESS. Last year we had no less than twenty-seven honeymoon couples—they all 'ad this room—separately, of course.

WIFE. Oh, Harry!

HUSBAND. That will be all now, thank you, Mrs. Blake.

PROPRIETRESS. Well—ring if you want anything, you know.

HUSBAND. Yes—thank you.

PROPRIETRESS (*roguishly*). I don't suppose you'll ring much though, will you?

WIFE. Oh, Harry!

HUSBAND. Oh, good night.

PROPRIETRESS (*laughing gaily*). It's me as should be saying that to you—sir.

(*She goes out door C.*)

WIFE. Oh, Harry! (WIFE *sits on sofa.*)

(*This whole scene to be played in an agony of embarrassment.*)

(HUSBAND *sits on sofa.*)

HUSBAND. Well—here we are.

WIFE. Yes—here we are.

HUSBAND. Quite a nice room, isn't it?

WIFE. Delightful.

HUSBAND. It all went off very well, didn't it?

WIFE. Yes.

HUSBAND. Yes, and now—er—well—here we are.

(HUSBAND *gets up from sofa.*)

WIFE. Yes—here we are.

HUSBAND. When we've unpacked we can put the bags under—the— (*he looks in agony at the bed*) sofa.

WIFE. Yes—we can—can't we?

HUSBAND. Yes—we can, can't we. Who's going to unpack first, you or me?

WIFE. I don't know.

HUSBAND. We'll toss up—tails you do—heads I do.

WIFE. Oh, Harry! (*Gets up from sofa—crosses to* HARRY.)

HUSBAND (*throwing coin*). It's heads—that's you!

WIFE. Oh!

HUSBAND. I'll—er—go downstairs and order breakfast for the morning—while you—er—get into—er—start to unpack.

WIFE. Very well.

HUSBAND (*kissing her hurriedly*). Cheer up, dear.

WIFE. Oh, Harry!

(*He goes out quickly.*)

(*She falls on her knees by the sofa.*)

(*Wailing.*) Oh, mother—oh, mother—oh, mother!

BLACK OUT

## SCENE II

*A very modern hotel bedroom.*

(*A* HUSBAND *and* WIFE *are ushered in by the* BOOKING CLERK. *A* PAGE BOY *enters with the luggage.*)

PROPRIETOR. I hope you'll be comfortable here.

WIFE. Oh yes—divine. (*She thumps the bed with her fist.*) Bed feels all right.

HUSBAND. Got a stinker on you?

WIFE. Yes—here—— (*She gives him one.*)

HUSBAND (*to* CLERK). Send up two dry Martinis, will you?

(*The* WIFE *opens a portable gramophone and puts on a dance record, then starts to undress.*)

WIFE. Here, Harry—unhook me.

HUSBAND (*doing so*). Right—Ouch!

WIFE. What is it?

HUSBAND. I always scratch myself with this damned hook!

BLACK OUT

## "IT DOESN'T MATTER HOW OLD YOU ARE"

1928

*Verse* 1

Life is just a gamble
And without preamble
I should like to state my case.
I'm no Messalina,
I've a slightly cleaner
Outlook on the human race.
Don't imagine that I'm hewn from
Marble or stone,
I'm not utterly immune from
Pangs of my own.
Tho' I'm over forty
I can still be naughty
In an unassuming way,
Beauty doesn't always win the day
I say.

*Refrain* 1

It doesn't matter how old you are
If the joys of life are sweet,
It doesn't matter how cold you are
If you've still got central heat.

I've seen raddled wrecks
With false pearls hung round their necks
Get away with lots of sex appeal,
And tho' I may have been through the mill
I'm a creature of passion still;
It doesn't matter how old you are,
It's just how young you feel.

*Verse 2*

Tho' I'm not a gay girl,
I'm a " come-what-may " girl,
Nothing in my life is planned.
Men with love get blinded,
But I'm so broad-minded
I just smile and understand.
Men don't always want to marry,
They're not to blame,
I'm quite certain that Du Barry
Felt just the same.
Too much love is nauseous,
One can't be too cautious
Cupid's such a wily foe;
Tho' I never let myself quite go
I know.

*Refrain 2*

It doesn't matter how old you are
If your heart can still beat fast,
It doesn't matter how bold you are
When the dangerous age is past.

Tho' my face is lined
And my outlook too refined
I shall never let my mind congeal.
Pompadour found her love a curse,
But I'll go further and fare much worse;
It doesn't matter how old you are,
It's just how young you feel.

*Refrain 3*

It doesn't matter how old you are
If you've still the strength to care,
However naughty you're told you are
It's entirely your affair.
Tho' I come a smack
And go rolling off the track
It will never be from lack of zeal.
You may laugh when you look at me,
But watch the papers and wait and see!
It doesn't matter how old you are,
It's just how young you feel.

## SHOP-GIRLS

1928

### CHARACTERS:

Lady Violet Angerville
The Hon. Muriel Petworth
Princess Panatelli
Lady Cicely Merle-Whidden
J. W. Vanderhoven
Vera, Duchess of Pangbourne

(*The scene is the showroom of Vera, Duchess of Pangbourne's furniture shop in Shepherd's Market. There are a few pieces of priced furniture, some knick-knacks and lengths of coloured brocades, chintzes and linoleums.*)

(*When the curtain rises it is about noon and* Muriel, Lady Violet *and* Lady Cicely *are mixing cocktails on a badly-pickled occasional table, from which is hanging a large price ticket.*)

Muriel (*shaking the shaker*). Phyllis was there, of course, looking terribly dazed.

Violet (*languidly*). She always does.

CICELY. One can't blame her, darling, she's had five children in three years.

VIOLET. And her husband died on Armistice Day.

MURIEL. So muddling. Oh!

(*The top comes off the shaker and everyone gets rather wet.*)

CICELY. Really, Muriel, why can't you be more careful. It's gone all over that brand new Jacobean table.

MURIEL. Such a pity it was pickled already.

(*They all laugh.*)

(*Enter* VERA, DUCHESS OF PANGBOURNE—*she is grey-haired and vague and hung with pearls.*)

VERA. Where's Blusie?

CICELY. He's at a sale trying to get a dresser for Lady Pinwright.

VERA. I thought she'd left the stage.

CICELY. Don't be silly, darling; not that sort of a dresser.

VERA (*glancing out of the window*). Give me a cocktail quickly, dear, there's a customer coming.

VIOLET (*devoutly*). Please God let it be an American.

CICELY (*anxiously to* MURIEL, *who is using a lipstick*). How's my hair, darling?

MURIEL. Just an old Kentish haystack, dear.

CICELY. Don't be so horrid. (*She rushes to mirror and scrutinizes herself.*) I look divine——

(J. W. VANDERHOVEN *enters. He is an insignificant looking American.* VERA *advances toward him.*)

VERA. How do you do?

VANDERHOVEN (*slightly surprised*). Pleased to meet you.

VERA. I'm sure we've met somewhere before—were you at that frightful party at Lady Dover's on Tuesday?

VANDERHOVEN. No, I got in on the *Leviathan* yesterday——

VERA. How marvellous! that's the one with those three divine red funnels, isn't it.

VANDERHOVEN. I should like to see some old tables if you have any——

VERA. We've got masses—Cicely, where's number 42?

CICELY. In the storehouse—one of its poor darling legs came off.

VERA. And Number 37?

CICELY. That's in the storehouse too, unless Blusie took it.

VERA. Where are the keys of the storehouse?

VIOLET. You had them last, dear.

VERA. No, I didn't, I remember distinctly giving them to Muriel.

MURIEL. What a terrible lie, Vera; you know perfectly well I only came back from Paris yesterday.

VERA. I gave them to you before you went to Paris.

VIOLET. We'll have to wire to Chanel, that's all.

VERA (*turning to* J. W.). There's this table, of course. It's rather fun, don't you think?

VANDERHOVEN. I'm afraid it's not quite big enough——

VERA. Of course, it all depends what you want it for, but personally I always think small tables are far more amusing than big ones.

(*The telephone rings and* CICELY *answers it.*)

CICELY. Hallo—yes—no, dear. I'd rather die. I've seen it five times already—I can't bear her, she always does cartwheels—all right—I'll ask her. (*To* VERA.) Are you going to Freda's to-night late?

VERA (*to* J. W.). We've got a heavenly old Queen Anne writing-table—— (*To* CICELY.) No, dear, I haven't forgiven her for her last party yet—— (*She takes* J. W. *over to a writing-table.*) You must say that's fun!

VANDERHOVEN. I'm afraid I don't want a writing-table.

CICELY (*at telephone*). Yes, darling—she'd adore to come—about 11.30? All right—— Byes——

(PRINCESS PANATELLI, *tall and wispy and very distracted, enters.*)

PRINCESS. Vera, what *has* happened to that little mother-of-pearl hair-tidy?

VERA. It was on top of Number 32 last Monday.

PRINCESS. It isn't there now—— (*She goes off aimlessly.*)

VERA. If you're furnishing a house you *must* look at our wall-papers—Cicely—wall-papers.

(CICELY *staggers over with a large book of modern wall-papers and plumps it down.*)

VERA. They are perfectly entrancing—they've only just arrived from Berlin—there (*she points to a pattern*), look at those absurd little roses. They almost make one forgive the Germans for the war, don't they?

VANDERHOVEN. I don't really need any wall-papers—you see—I have a great deal of old oak.

VERA. Pickled?

VANDERHOVEN (*offended*). I beg your pardon.

VERA. Is it pickled?

VANDERHOVEN. No—no—I'm afraid it's not.

VERA. Well, you must let us pickle it for you immediately——

(*The telephone rings.*)

Old oak now, let me see—— I have the most divine little prie-Dieu which would be grand fun for the dining-room——

CICELY (*at telephone*). Yes—she's here—— Vera! Cogie wants you—— (*She hands her the telephone.*)

VERA. Excuse me for a moment—hello Cogie, darling, what a surprise! I thought you were in the Isle of Wight—— No!—I couldn't be more pleased—of course—it's not true! She was all right on Friday, but drinking heavily—poor dear—very well—yes, darling—no, I won't say a word—about 7.15—— Byes—— Violet, do you know that on Sunday morning Marion drove straight up the steps of the Victoria Memorial?

VIOLET. *Lèse majesté,* darling.

VERA (*to* J. W.). Do you know Marion Wendle?

VANDERHOVEN. No, I'm afraid I don't.

VERA. Well, if you did I don't suppose you'd recognize her now—what were we saying?

VANDERHOVEN. I think if you don't mind I'll come back another day when you're less busy.

VERA. Nonsense, we're not in the *least* busy—where is your house?

VANDERHOVEN. South Audley Street.

VERA. Just near the Croughboroughs? Do you know the Croughboroughs?

VANDERHOVEN. No, I'm afraid I——

VERA. But you *must*. They *are* such fun. Mustn't he know the Croughboroughs, Violet?

VIOLET. Of course he must——

(*Re-enter* PRINCESS PANATELLI.)

PRINCESS. I'm so terribly worried about that little mother-of-pearl hair-tidy.

(*She wanders off.*)

VANDERHOVEN. I think, if you don't mind——

VERA. Are you quite sure you don't want this little table?

VANDERHOVEN (*seeing a way of escape*). Yes—yes—— I'll have that—how much is it?

VERA. Seventy pounds.

VANDERHOVEN (*looking at the price-ticket*). It says fifteen on this.

VERA (*quickly*). That's the number—we have everything numbered, you know. It's so much more business-like.

VIOLET (*kissing* VERA). I must fly, darling. I've got to go and see the young man.

(*She goes out.*)

VANDERHOVEN (*suddenly seeing a very impressionistic painting*). What's this?

VERA. That's a Pustontin.

VANDERHOVEN. A what?

VERA. Pustontin—he's a modern of the moderns, you know.

VANDERHOVEN. What's it supposed to be?

VERA. No one knows—that's what's such agony—it's fourth dimensional, of course—abstract painting. I think he does it with his feet—he designs a lot for us, but, of course, he's wildly expensive.

(*Re-enter* PRINCESS PANATELLI.)

PRINCESS. Vera, I'm dreadfully upset.

VERA. What *is* the matter?

PRINCESS. I don't care what you say—someone must have taken it.

VERA. What?

PRINCESS (*wailing*). That darling little mother-of-pearl hair-tidy!

VERA. Let's see, who's been in—now——

PRINCESS. Olga came yesterday afternoon——

VERA. Well, it's our own fault, we owe her twenty pounds commission.

(*The* PRINCESS *wanders off*.)

VANDERHOVEN. Well, good morning.

VERA. I can't dream of allowing you to go until you see our brocades—lovely brocades—they're too marvellous for words—all hand done.

(CICELY *brings some lengths of brocade, which* VERA *spreads out*.)

There! Isn't that entrancing? What colours! Are you having any colour in your drawing-room?

VANDERHOVEN. I haven't decided yet really.

VERA. Well, let's decide now—it will be grand fun—what about that lovely bright dustman green with curtains of this?

VANDERHOVEN. I'd really prefer something simpler, I think.

VERA. Well, if you want simplicity, why not have the whole thing sand colour with just one or two cushions of this?

VANDERHOVEN. Would that be expensive in cushions?

VERA. No, no, not at all. Dirt cheap.

VANDERHOVEN. How much, roughly?

VERA. Oh, about ten pounds each.

VANDERHOVEN. I see. (*He puts out his hand to take the price-ticket, and is just looking at it when she snatches it from him.*) What's that?

VERA (*slightly flurried*). That's nothing, just the designer's name.

VANDERHOVEN. Designer?

VERA. Yes—one of our greatest decorative artists, Bourne and Hollingsworth!

## TRIO: "BACK TO NATURE"

1928

*Verse* I

ALL. WE'RE here to make confession,
We're forming a triple alliance,
Our years of drab repression
Have burst into open defiance.
We've bid good-bye to faces dear
And mother-in-laws and wives.
We now intend to disappear
And reconstruct our lives.

*Refrain* I

ALL. We're over-civilised,
That's the trouble with us.
Our hearts of pickled oak
Are casting off the yoke.
Tho' we are under-sized
We're not giving a cuss,
We're striking off the chains to-day.

1ST. We find that the town
Is keeping us down,
We're yearning to expand.

2ND. For life in a bank
Is dingy and dank,
It's more than we can stand.

3RD. We mean to abscond
Into the beyond
And roll in blood and sand.
ALL. We're going back to nature right away.

*Verse 2*

ALL. The climate rules the nation,
The temperature's rapidly falling,
With over-population
The squalor of life is appalling.
We're tired of trying year by year
To imitate plaster saints,
We mean to change our atmosphere
And lose our self-restraints.

*Refrain 2*

ALL. We're too respectable,
That's what's holding us back,
We lie and dream at nights
Of primitive delights.
Think how delectable
Life would be in a shack
With nobody to say us nay.
3RD. I'll jump on my horse,
Side-saddle, of course,
And ride across the green.
1ST. I'll gallop and shoot
And plunder and loot
With none to intervene.
2ND. As quick as a wink
I'll carelessly drink
A pail of Ovaltine.
ALL. We're going back to nature right away!

*Verse 3*

ALL. We must admit the movies
Have helped to complete our damnation.
Now what we want to prove is
Our utter demoralisation.
We don't intend to waste our time
With celibacy and such,
We'll lead a life of social crime
And like it very much.

*Refrain 3*

ALL. We're too adaptable
That's what's wrong with us now.
There must be hidden charms
In North Canadian farms.
We've never slapped a bull,
Never sworn at a cow,
We can't distinguish straw from hay,
2ND. But nevertheless,
I'm bound to confess,
I'm full of do and dare.
3RD. If life is a bore
I'll hire a squaw,
With charming savoir faire,
1ST. Where women are bold
And quite uncontrolled
All in the open air.
ALL. We're going back to nature right away!

## "WHAT LOVE MEANS TO GIRLS LIKE ME"

1922

*Verse* I

A little word,
Four letters only,
And yet it means a lot you must admit.
It seems absurd
But when I'm lonely
I lose my sense of values just a bit.
If men are really willing
I must say I find it thrilling
Just to listen to the charming things they say,
Though I'm not exactly fickle
In a quiet unassuming sort of way.

*Refrain* I

It isn't that I'm naughty or capricious,
It isn't that I single out my prey.
I'm sure I have a mind,
Too essentially refined,
To flaunt my girlish charms in any way.
I sometimes think that Eve was very thoughtless

To wrench the fruit of knowledge from the tree,
More abstemious she'd have been,
Could she only have foreseen
What loves means to girls like me.

*Verse 2*

If love is blind,
And people say so,
I'm certain that that statement's incorrect.
I shouldn't mind
If he would stay so,
It's when he starts to see things I object.
To say that Cupid hates me,
And deliberately bates me,
Would really not exaggerate the case.
You could wheel away in barrows
All the bleeding, blunted arrows
That from time to time he's fired in my face.

*Refrain 2*

It isn't that I'm thoroughly degraded,
It isn't that I go from bad to worse,
It isn't that I pine
For roses, love and wine.
I'm the victim of a temperamental curse,
I often try to suffocate my passion
Though all the time I yearn to set it free.
Cleopatra, at her best,
Would have shuddered if she'd guessed
What love means to girls like me.

*Refrain 3*

It isn't that I'm consciously alluring,
It isn't that I'm altogether bad.
  A girl may have her dreams,
  Without going to extremes,
Though I shouldn't like to mention some I've had.
It isn't that I take all and give nothing,
I'm sure I'm generous-hearted as can be,
  But poor Mary Queen of Scots
  Would have tied herself in knots
For what love means to girls like me.

## LAW AND ORDER

1928

(*The scene is a street in London. This is a cloth painted with park railings and a lamp-post R.*)

(POLICEWOMAN PELLET *enters from right—advances to centre of stage, bends and straightens herself in traditional fashion and stands left of lamp-post. An* OLD WOMAN, *selling matches, enters from left—walks across and meets* P.W. PELLET.)

PELLET. Move on—you're loitering.

OLD WOMAN. I can't move any faster—I've got fallen arches. (*Spits.*)

PELLET. Don't argue, don't argue. You're loitering. Move on. (*Sniffs.*)

(*The* OLD WOMAN *goes off* 1 *E.R.*)

(PELLET *sniffs and stands still—a* GIRL *enters from right, walks to the middle of the stage—stoops down to tie her shoe lace. A* YOUNG MAN *enters also from right and bumps into her.*)

MAN. I beg your pardon.

GIRL. Not at all.

(*The* Man *goes off left and*—P.W. Wendle *strides on* I *E.L.*)

Wendle. Now then, now then——

Girl. What d'you mean "Now then"?

Wendle. None of that.

Girl. None of what?

Wendle. None of what you were thinking of.

Girl. How dare you! (*Crosses to left*).

Wendle. I've been watching you—flouncing about.

Girl. Don't you talk to me like that or I shall call a policeman.

(*She marches off with her head in the air.*)

Wendle. Impertinence!

Pellet (*sympathetically*). They're all alike. The girls of to-day—fast, overdressed, *and* saucy!

Wendle. I don't know what London's coming to—the higher the buildings the lower the morals.

Pellet. Been in the Force long?

Wendle. About three months—my husband went to Australia.

Pellet. On business?

Wendle. No, on purpose.

Pellet. It's the woman who pays, and pays.

Both. And pays.

Pellet. Men are all alike.

Wendle. Only some more than others. I'm not a suspicious woman, but I don't think my husband 'as been entirely faithful to me.

Pellet. Whatever makes you think that?

Wendle. My last child doesn't resemble him in the least.

PELLET. What you must have gone through.

WENDLE. Bottles and bottles—of aspirin.

PELLET (*producing paper bag*). 'Ave a choc?

WENDLE. Not on duty.

PELLET. Come on—there's no one about.

WENDLE. Well, as long as they 'aven't nut on 'em. (*She takes one.*)

(*They both munch.*)

(*There is a loud bang off stage.*)

PELLET. What was that?

WENDLE. Only one of them balloon tyres burst.

PELLET. I see the Croydon Ramblers beat the Lyons' Corner House girls last Tuesday.

WENDLE. No stamina in that Lyons lot.

PELLET. Oh, I don't know—Minnie Packer's a lovely centre forward.

WENDLE. She had to leave the field.

PELLET. Why?

WENDLE. Lost 'er bust bodice in a scrum.

PELLET. Go on!

WENDLE. Lily Burton finished the game—and you know what she is—all hips and hysteria.

PELLET. I wish I'd been there—I 'ad to do extra duty—Vera Pearn got special leave to go to the white sales.

WENDLE. Favouritism.

PELLET. I gave Inspector Rogers a piece of my mind, I can tell you.

WENDLE. She's a mean cat, that Inspector Rogers, if ever there was one.

PELLET. And common!—— My dear—do you know she——

(*They draw closer*—PELLET *whispers.*)

WENDLE. She *didn't!*

PELLET. She did—right in me face.

WENDLE. What did you do?

PELLET. I saluted and swept out—but I couldn't 'elp crying a bit when I got me 'elmet off. But luckily Sergeant Leggat came in and she lent me 'er puff and we got to talking. She told me all about Jessie Lucas.

WENDLE. What about her?

PELLET. She's in 'ospital.

WENDLE. What—again!

PELLET. No. She was on duty at Victoria Station and got three ribs broken trying to see Adolphe Menjou.

WENDLE. Adolphe Menjou?

PELLET. I love Adolphe Menjou—he's so suave.

WENDLE. He's suave right enough, but I prefer Ronald Colman—he's more bellicose—don't misunderstand, I mean more up and doing. Did you see that film—John Gilbert and Greta Garbo?

PELLET. My dear! After the first kiss I quivered like an aspurn.

WENDLE. They oughtn't to do it, you know—it's past a joke. After all, we're only human——

(*Both bend.*)

PELLET. Do you remember that robe de nuit she wore?

WENDLE. The one with the black chiffon?

PELLET. Yes, I saw the spitting image of it in Swan and Edgar's.

WENDLE. Did you get it?

PELLET (*giggling*). Well, I know it was terribly naughty of me, but I just couldn't resist it.

WENDLE. Is it cut V-shape?—too divine!——

PELLET. Well, dear, I must say I 'ad to alter it a bit——

(*Shouts off right.*)

WENDLE. See your skin through it——

(*Their conversation is here lost in a terrible commotion off stage. Shouts and screams of "Murder." A* MAN *rushes across the stage clutching a knife, followed by* TWO WOMEN *screaming and another* MAN *brandishing a revolver.* PELLET *and* WENDLE *are so engrossed that they don't see them—when the* FOUR PEOPLE *have gone off there is suddenly a loud, single scream and a shot.*)

PELLET. What was that?

WENDLE. Only another one of those tyres burst.

BLACK OUT

## TRY TO LEARN TO LOVE

1928

(Boy *and* Girl *enter* 1 *E.R. Dance as arranged.*)

*Verse* 1

He. In kindergartens,
In country or town,
Our education begins,
Like little Spartans
We're taught to crush down
The inclination to sin.
When we change to gentle adolescence
Things get rather strained.
There's a strange, peculiar effervescence
No one has explained.

*Chorus* 1. (*Repeat*)

First you learn to spell a little bit,
Then, if you excel a little bit,
Other things as well a little bit
Come our way;
Though the process may be slow to you
Knowledge of the world will flow to you.
Steadily you grow a little bit,
Day by day;

Though you're too gentle, sentimental
In fact, quite a dreary bore,
Though you're æsthetic, apathetic,
To all men but Bernard Shaw,
Use the velvet glove a little bit,
Emulate a dove a little,
Try to learn to love a little bit more.

*Verse 2*

SHE. The art of wooing,
I'm firmly resolved,
For men is terribly crude.
To be pursuing
Is not so involved
As having to be pursued.
Doubts and fears
Make woman work much faster,
Tho' they're frail and weak,
Taking years
Successfully to master
Feminine technique.

*Refrain 2*

First you droop your eyes—a little bit,
Then if you are wise—a little bit,
Register surprise—a little bit,
If he's bold,
Stamp your foot with some celerity,
Murmur with intense sincerity
That his immature temerity
Leaves you cold.

But when you get him
You must let him
Have the joy he's yearning for,
And whisper sweetly
Indiscreetly
He's the boy that you adore.
Use the moon above a little bit,
Emulate the dove a little bit
Try to learn to love—a little bit more.

TABS OPEN

(*They dance one chorus and—Exit 2 E.L.*)

(CHORUS *enter from 2 E.R., sing first refrain as they come on. Dance as arranged—Exit 2 E.R.*)

(BOY *and* GIRL *enter 1 E.L., dance to two choruses as arranged.*)

CLOSE TABS AT END OF DANCE

# CHAUVE SOURIS

1928

## Introduction

*Speech before Curtain*

Ladies and gentlemen, ass you see I find him verrey deeficult to spik Eenglish. There iss an old Russian proberb wheech say that a dead rhinosceros iss nearer to the starrs than a leetle child who steecks a peen eento iss old grandmother, all of wheech have no bearing whatever upon the leetle scene wheech my Company weel preesent.

Eet iss a peecneeck een olt Russia. The caviare iss all up eaten and the samovar dry and the peasants play peculiar games weeth one another and seeng and seeng and seeng.

## Open with Music

*Quintette*

(*Profile Boat*—Four Men *and* One Woman *standing behind it. They are dressed in burlesque Russian costumes.*)

Ish con broshka,
Whoops dad illoshka,
Whoops dad illoshka,
Inkle drop vaard.

Ish con broshka,
Whoops dad illoshka,
Whoops dad illoshka,
Inkle drop vaard.

Wheeshka eeglee,
Wheeshka bombolom,
Wheeshka weedlewee,
Chock chock wish laa.

Wheeshka eeglee,
Wheeshka bombolom,
Wheeshka weedlewee,
Inkle drop vaard.

TABS CLOSE ON LAST NOTE

(ANNOUNCER *comes from Centre, bows to audience.*)

ANNOUNCER. I hope you have liked him and will tell all your friends about her—and ask them all to came.

(*Exits through Centre.*)

# THE LEGEND OF THE LILY OF THE VALLEY

1928

## DRESS PLOT

FLANNELETTE. Beaded Shaftesbury Avenue evening frock, necklace of ping-pong balls—brown leather aviator's cap, cricket pads and bare feet.

BERGAMOT. American Union two-piece bathing suit, bare legs ; boots with spats and an admiral's hat—bow and arrow.

FEMALE COURTIERS. Pink flannel drawers, lace camisoles, Russian boots. The framework of hoop skirts composed of gas piping—head-dress traditional of eighteenth century with dolls' furniture festooned in the hair.

MALE COURTIERS. Jaeger long-legged combinations—football boots—brass-studded leather belts, with small jewelled swords—small gold crowns on elastic.

FAIRIES. Burberrys, bowler hats, long rope wigs reaching to the floor—gossamer wings—pink satin ballet shoes.

MARQUIS DE POOPINAC. Plus fours—Harlequin shirt with spangles, tight-fitting cap with a celluloid windmill. Bare legs with carpet slippers.

## INTRODUCTORY SPEECH

Ladies and gentlemen, as a sop to those of you who are bored and satiated with usual superficialities of light musical entertainments, Mr. Cochran has asked me to announce the production of a short ballet in which beauty, austerity and intellectuality are blended together with that spirit of progressive modernity which we have learned to demand and expect from the striking performances of Diaghelieff's Russian Ballet. We live in an age of Revolution in Art and perhaps the most vital and tremendous movement in this revolution is the stern reversion to bare primitive simplicity.

The ballet we are about to present is entitled "The Legend of the Lily of the Valley." The atmosphere is definitely early eighteenth century, French, smacking of gently undulating country life, and then again, smacking ever so slightly of the debauched life at Court. The actual legend is simplicity itself. Flannelette, a dainty shepherdess of the period, is guarding her flock; occasionally she dances to them, but they pay no heed—suddenly from over the hill comes striding Bergamot, a shepherd who loves her. They execute what is technically described as a Pas de Deux, which leaves Flannelette exhausted—Bergamot plays his pipe to her for a moment and then goes sadly away. Flannelette is left dreaming on the grass, during which the love theme is repeated in the orchestra for three flutes and the cophatican. Then six fairies enter and execute with considerable spirit a Pas du Tout—Flannelette starts up amazed——Suddenly a bugle call is heard. The fairies rush off and a coach drives by—stops, and disgorges the evil and depraved Marquis de Poopinac with several Court ladies, whose tinkling false laughter sounds strangely incongruous in such sylvan surroundings. This jarring note is brought out in the music with astounding effect by a muted oboe and six clavabaladalas. The Marquis, observing Flannelette, is immediately inflamed by her beauty. He flirts with her, and she, flattered by his attention, accompanies him to a neighbouring coppice, during which the courtiers dance a stately Pavanne, which is interrupted by the re-entrance of Bergamot, who is searching wildly for Flannelette—he questions each of the courtiers in mime, or dumb show, but they only laugh mockingly—suddenly a cry is heard. Flannelette comes running in with her fichu extremely ruffled, followed by the Marquis. Bergamot attacks him, and the Marquis runs him through with his sword, and the story closes to music of transcendental beauty.

OPEN BLUE WITH MUSIC

# THE TUBE

1928

## CHARACTERS:

Bank Clerk
Lift Man
Fred
Harry
Lady Gwendoline Verney
The Hon. Millicent Bloodworthy
Charles
Mary
1st Girl
2nd Girl, Etc.
Urchin

(*The scene is the booking-office of an underground railway station. There is a newspaper stand on the left and on the right on an angle up stage are the lift gates, which are closed.*)

(Three People *come on quite quietly—buy papers and tickets at the slot machines, then take their stand by the lift. They open their papers and read them—a*

DIRTY LITTLE URCHIN *enters, gets a ticket and also takes his stand, then gradually two by two and in groups the entire company come on (with the exception of a few principals required in the ensuing scene). All buy papers and tickets and queue up waiting for the lift. Everyone is completely preoccupied and dressed in ordinary workaday clothes, and there should be no sound at all but the click of the slot machine and the rustle of newspapers. Suddenly the little* URCHIN, *who has been unable to afford a paper, begins to whistle through his teeth—quite softly at first. One or two people lower their papers and regard him rather impatiently for a moment—the tune he is whistling is a very definite dance rhythm—he whistles a little louder—a woman a few feet away from him, without looking up, begins to shuffle her feet unconsciously. The man with her stops her with an irritable nudge. The* URCHIN *continues to whistle—an elderly business man immersed in his paper begins to shuffle his feet—then the woman starts again—gradually as the boy's whistle gets louder, everyone starts moving slightly—the man at the bookstall takes up the tune and hums it carelessly, then almost imperceptibly at first, the orchestra takes up the tune—it swells louder until everybody is dancing hard. At this moment a young* BANK CLERK *rushes in hurriedly, buys a ticket and a paper—looks at everyone jigging about—recognizes the tune and sings it.)*

(BANK CLERK *sings one verse, one chorus.* BANK CLERK *and* CHORUS *sing one chorus, and into* DANCE *as arranged.)*

### *" Waiting in a Queue "*

*Verse*

In a rut
In a rut
In a rut
We go along.
Nothing but
Nothing but
Nothing but
The same old song.
To those who view us lightly
We must seem slightly
Absurd.
We never break the ritual
One habitual
Herd.

*Refrain*

Waiting in a queue
Waiting in a queue
Everybody's always waiting in a queue.
Fat and thin
They all begin
To take their stand—it's grand—queueing it.
Everywhere you go
Everywhere you go
Everybody's always standing in a row.
Short and tall
And one and all
The same as sheep—just keep—doing it.
No one says why
No one says how

No one says what is this for.
No one says no
No one says go
No one says this is a bore.
If you want to do
Anything that's new,
If you're feeling happy, furious or blue,
Wet or fine
You get in line,
For everybody's waiting in a queue.

(*At the end of the Number the lift comes up—the* ATTENDANT *dances out and* EVERYONE *dances in, the* YOUNG MAN *and the* ATTENDANT *last. The gates close and the lift disappears and the* MAN *in the bookstall stops humming as the rhythm dies away in the orchestra.*)

(*Enter* 1 E.R. LADY GWENDOLYN VERNEY *and* THE HON. MILLICENT BLOODWORTHY, *elaborately and expensively dressed. They look round, slightly bewildered.*)

LADY G. What do we do now, darling?

MILLICENT. Get our tickets, I suppose.

LADY G. Yes, but where? Life's agony, isn't it?

MILLICENT. Torture, dear—but it's no use grumbling—we can't possibly use our cars with all the roads up—we must just be brave and do what the common people do.

LADY G. It all seems very complicated. (*Turns and sees ticket machines.*) Look at these funny grey things!

MILLICENT. Those must be the ticket machines.

LADY G. My dear, how delicious! We must put in some pennies, or something.

MILLICENT. I haven't any change.

LADY G. Neither have I. We'll get it at the book-stall.

MILLICENT (*crosses to news-stand*). Have you got "*Vogue*"?

(FRED *is in front of newspaper stand.*)

FRED. 'Ave I got wot?

MILLICENT. *Vogue.*

FRED. Wot's that?

LADY G. It's a paper, I'm afraid.

FRED. I got *Tit Bits, Answers,* an' all the "dailies."

MILLICENT. Have you change for a pound?

FRED. Mostly in pennies, mum.

LADY G. How divine—we can buy things with them.

FRED. I shouldn't do that, ma'am, if I was you. I should send them to the British Museum as curiosities. (*Goes to back of stall and gets change.*)

MILLICENT. Here's the pound.

FRED (*counting out change*). There y'are, lady. There's three and six in coppers, five and five's ten, and ten's a pound.

MILLICENT. Thank you a thousand times.

FRED. It's a pleasure, so 'elp me God.

LADY G. Come along, darling (*crosses to machines*).

MILLICENT (*putting a penny in the ticket machine*). It's really quite an adventure, isn't it?

(*The ticket comes out.*)

LADY G. I'm thrilled—we must have some more—— (*She puts in several pennies.*)

MILLICENT (*also cramming pennies in*). What tremendous fun!

FRED. 'Ere, 'ere, 'ere, wot you think you're doing? (*He comes over to the machine.*)

LADY G. I'm afraid it's stuck.

FRED. This ain't Wembley, you know. (*He shakes the machine.*)

MILLICENT. There now—I've got fourteen. How many have you, darling?

LADY G. I've got tons.

FRED. Wot's the idea? That's what I want to know. Wot's the idea? Where d'yer want to go?

LADY G. Well, we want ultimately to get to the Ritz.

FRED (*crosses to R. shouting*). 'Arry, 'Arry, come 'ere!

HARRY. 'Allo!

(HARRY, *the booking-clerk, comes out of his office and comes to centre.*)

What's the matter?

FRED. 'Ere's a couple of bejewelled duchesses bunging up one of the "'ow-d'yer-do's."

HARRY (*shaking the machine*). What d'you want to come mucking about 'ere for? You ought to be at home looking after your children.

MILLICENT. We happen to be unmarried.

FRED. I shouldn't 'ave thought you'd let a little thing like that stand in yer way.

LADY G. Horrible brute!

FRED. Who's 'orrible?

MILLICENT. Come away, Gwen dear, they're insulting us.

(*Goes off* I *E.L.*)

LADY G. There are your ridiculous tickets!

(*She throws them over both the* MEN *and goes out grandly* I *E.L.*)

HARRY. Well, I'll be damned!

FRED. There you are—that's class.

HARRY. Class, phew! If my old woman made up 'er eyes like that, I'd lock 'er in the scullery!

FRED. Wot do they want to come nosing round 'ere for—bloated aristocrats.

HARRY. You know the trouble with you, Fred, is you're a bit Bolshie.

Fred. No, all this democracy makes life 'ellish uncomfortable.

HARRY. What we want in England is more and better birth control.

FRED. Oh no, we don't.

HARRY. Oh yes we do.

FRED. It's men like you as is responsible for the birth-rate falling.

HARRY. Well, if you're responsible for it rising, you ought to be ashamed of yourself. This country's over-populated.

(*Enter* CHARLES, *a very exquisite young man. Crosses to centre, looks at them and then goes up to ticket machines.*)

FRED. No, it ain't. It's all right—you've won. I'm all for birth control.

(CHARLES *puts a penny in the slot machine and cannot work it.*)

CHARLES. I say!—attendant—it's stuck.

(*Lift rises.*)

FRED. Give it a shake.

(CHARLES *shakes it gently.*)

CHARLES. I'm afraid it's still stuck.

(*Lift doors open.—Exit two people R. and L.*)

FRED. I said shake it—not stroke it! 'Ere! (FRED *comes over to machine.*) Where d'you want to go—anyhow?

CHARLES. Queen's Gate.

(FRED *gives the machine a violent shake—gets ticket out, gives it to* CHARLES, *then pushes him into the lift.*)

FRED. Take him away, Hubert—'e's breaking my 'eart.

LIFT MAN. Right!

(*The lift goes down.*)

FRED. 'Arry, that's wot the Russian Ballet's done for England.

(MARY *enters* I *E.R. She is charmingly dressed and she is reading a book in which she is so engrossed that she collides with* FRED, *who has crossed to R.C.*)

MARY. Oh, I *am* so sorry.

FRED. That's all right, miss.

MARY. Could you tell me the time, please?

FRED. About eleven o'clock.

MARY. Thank you, it doesn't matter if I wait here for a little, does it? (*Crosses to centre.*)

FRED. You can wait here as long as you like.

(TWO GIRLS *come on from* 1 *E.L., buy tickets, and wait for the lift.*)

MARY. I'm expecting a friend.

FRED. Boy friend, I'll be bound.

MARY. You're quite right.

(1ST GIRL *suddenly sees* MARY *and crosses to L. of her.*)

1ST GIRL. Mary!

MARY. Hallo!

1ST GIRL. What are you doing here?

MARY. I'm waiting for Jack Burton.

2ND GIRL. Jack! We've just left him——

MARY. Oh! Perhaps I mistook the time——

1ST GIRL. Didn't you have a row with him last night?

MARY. Yes—but not a serious one.

2ND GIRL. Are you sure?

1ST GIRL. You're so difficult, you know—you won't be content with men as they are—you're always trying to alter them.

MARY. Only because they never seem a bit like what they're made out to be in books.

1ST GIRL. Books! Who cares about books?

MARY. I do.

(*Lift rises.*)

2ND GIRL (*crosses to R.*) Life comes first, duckie. If I were you, I'd step out of my beautiful dreamland and face a bit of reality—it's more comforting in the long run.

MARY. You think I'm a fool, don't you?

(*Lift doors open—exit* TWO PEOPLE.)

2ND GIRL. Not exactly—but you're always pretending things are what they're not.

1ST GIRL. Here's the lift. Good-bye, Mary.

MARY. Good-bye.

(*They enter lift and it goes down.*)

CLOSE NO. 1 TABS

NUMBER

" *Mary Make-Believe* "

*Verse*

I have been reading in this book of mine
  About a foolish maiden's prayer,
And every gesture, word and look of mine
  Seems to be mirrored there.
She had such terribly pedantic dreams
That her romantic schemes
  Went all awry,
Her thoughts were such
She claimed too much
  And true love passed her by.

*Refrain*

Mary make-believe
  Dreamed the whole day through
    Foolish fancies,
    Love romances,
  How could they come true?
Mary make-believe
  Sighed a little up her sleeve,
    Nobody claimed her,

They only named her
Mary Make-Believe.

(*During this Refrain* EIGHT GIRLS *enter from* 1 *E.R. and* EIGHT *from* 1 *E.L.*)

*Counter melody to be sung by* CHORUS

She's just a girl who's always blowing mental bubbles
Till she's quite out of breath—quite out of breath.
She seems to have the knack of magnifying troubles
Till they crush her to death—crush her to death.
She's just a duffer of the ineffective kind,
She's bound to suffer from her introspective mind,
Her indecisions quite prevent her visions—coming true,
Imagination is a form of flagellation,
If a sensitive child—lets it run wild
It dims the firmament till all the world is permanently blue.
She's simply bound to make a bloomer
Until she's found her sense of humour.
If love should touch her ever
She'll never, never see it through.

(*And* MARY *sings the Refrain at the same time* CHORUS *sing counter melody.*)

(DANCE *as arranged.*)

(*As* CHORUS *exit*—8 *R. and* 8 *L.*)

(MARY *is in centre of stage.*)

(FADE OUT *as* GIRLS *exit.*)

CLOSE TABS ON MARY'S LAST NOTE

## GROWING PAINS

1927

CHARACTERS:

PAPA
MAMMA
HERBERT

*The atmosphere and period are mid-Victorian. The scene is a refined English home.*

(MAMMA *with chignon and bustle is discovered weeping while* PAPA *with mutton-chop whiskers towers over her.*)

PAPA. The boy must be told.

MAMMA. Humphrey—Humphrey.

PAPA. He has reached the age of—of——

MAMMA. But only with the greatest care, Humphrey.

PAPA. There comes a time when a mother's tender solicitude must give place to a father's worldly influence.

MAMMA. My son—my son. (*She weeps again.*)

PAPA. Where is the lad?

MAMMA. Learning his Collect for Sunday.

PAPA. Call him.

MAMMA. But, Humphrey——

PAPA (*sternly*). Call him, Marion—and be brave.

MAMMA (*going to the door*). Herbert!—Herbert!—Your father wishes to speak to you. Oh, Humphrey, Humphrey—he is my babe, my unsullied blossom—I cannot bear it.

PAPA. Life is life, Marion—the boy must be told.

(HERBERT *comes running in—he is a well-grown lad, dressed à la little Lord Fauntleroy. He is sucking a pink sweet on a small stick.*)

HERBERT. You call me, Mamma?

MAMMA. Herbert—I—we—your father—oh dear—oh dear—oh dear! (*She goes out weeping.*)

HERBERT. Poor Mamma! She seems slightly hysterical this morning.

PAPA. Herbert!

HERBERT. Yes, Papa.

PAPA. Be seated.

HERBERT. Very well, Papa. (*He sits down.*)

PAPA. The time has come, Herbert, for you to be informed of certain facts of life which hitherto have been veiled from you.

HERBERT (*with a leer*). Yes, Papa?

PAPA. You have reached an age when—er——

HERBERT. Oh yes, Papa.

PAPA. I feel that my duty as a father towards you lies in the—er—revelation of—er—er——

HERBERT. Yes, Papa.

PAPA. Put that sweet down.

HERBERT (*laying it on the table*). Very well, Papa.

PAPA (*clearing his throat nervously*). There are in life, Herbert, certain strange elements which as a growing lad it is only right for you to know—for instance——

HERBERT (*smiling*). Go on, Papa.

PAPA. For instance—er—you may often have wondered during your childish frolics in the garden and in the meadows—how the—er—flowers and—er—birds——

HERBERT. Oh yes, Papa. (*He takes up the sweet again.*)

PAPA. Well, Herbert, I will go even further.

HERBERT. Very well, Papa.

PAPA. Has it ever occurred to you to question the appearance of a flock of tiny golden chicks or a young calf or a——

HERBERT (*wriggling delightedly*). Go on, Papa.

PAPA. Stop sucking that sweet.

HERBERT. Yes, Papa. (*He puts it down again.*)

PAPA. Where was I?

HERBERT. It's not for me to say, Papa.

PAPA (*pompously*). Your mother and I, Herbert——

HERBERT (*leaning forward*). Oh, Papa!

PAPA. Your mother and I have decided after a great deal of thought that there are certain facts of life which should be made clear to you.

HERBERT. You've said that before, Papa.

PAPA (*irritably*). Never mind whether I've said it before or whether I have not said it before—that is not the point.

HERBERT. What is the point, Papa?

PAPA (*clearing his throat again*). The point is this, Herbert—have you ever noticed a litter of little pigs in the sty——?

HERBERT (*with slight boredom*). Oh yes, Papa. (*He takes his sweet again.*)

PAPA. And, Herbert—has it ever occurred to you to ask yourself—er—er——

HERBERT. I'm waiting, Papa.

PAPA. The little pigs—er—grow and grow and grow until one day they—er—become—er—big pigs.

HERBERT (*eagerly*). What then, Papa?

PAPA. When they are big pigs they are sometimes sold and killed for bacon and—er—sometimes they are—er—not killed.

HERBERT. Obviously, Papa.

PAPA. And the ones that are not killed sometimes—er——

HERBERT. Go on, Papa.

PAPA. Will you stop sucking that filthy sweet!

(*He snatches it out of his hand and throws it across the room.*)

HERBERT. Why are you so nervous, Papa?

PAPA. I am not in the least nervous, Herbert, but that which I have to tell you is rather delicate—and—er—rather difficult.

HERBERT. What is that you want to tell me, Papa?

PAPA (*with a gulp*). My boy—there is no Santa Claus!

BLACK OUT

## THE ORDER OF THE DAY

1928

*The scene is a front cloth of a street with, on the right, three steps leading to the front door of a neat little house.*

(*The* HUSBAND *and* WIFE *come out—he is wearing a business suit, bowler hat, etc., and carrying a little bag.*)

WIFE. Well, good-bye, dear.

HUSBAND. Good-bye.

WIFE. Be home in good time for dinner.

HUSBAND. I always am.

WIFE. Have you got everything?

HUSBAND. Yes—everything. Good-bye. (*He kisses her and—walks off L.*)

(*When she has waved to him she goes into the house and comes out again with a pail of water and a scrubbing brush—she kneels down with her back to the audience and proceeds to scrub the steps—the* HUSBAND *comes on again L. tapping his pockets, obviously having forgotten something—he sees his wife—smiles—and, meaning to surprise her, creeps gaily up behind her and gives her a playful slap.*)

WIFE (*without turning her head*). Only half a pint this morning, Mr. Jones.

BLACK OUT

## "SOME DAY I'LL FIND YOU"

1930

*Verse 1*

When one is lonely the days are long,
    You seem so near
    But never appear
Each night I sing you a lover's song.
    Please try to hear,
    My dear, my dear.

*Verse 2*

Can't you remember the fun we had?
    Time is so fleet,
    Why shouldn't we meet?
When you're away from me days are so sad,
    Life's not complete,
    My sweet, my sweet.

Some day I'll find you,
Moonlight behind you.
True to the dream I am dreaming,
As I draw near you
You'll smile a little smile.

For a little while
We shall stand
Hand in hand.
I'll leave you never,
Love you for ever,
All our past sorrow redeeming.
Hear me not in vain,
Let the dream remain.
Some day I'll find you again.

# PARODY OF "PRIVATE LIVES"

1930

## Note

The following is a burlesque of the second act of "Private Lives."

The circumstances are the same as those in the play, except that the characters are drawn from the poorer and less cultured sections of society.

The scene is a furnished sitting-room in a lower middle-class lodging house; a deal table, on which are bread, cheese, pickles, bottled beer, etc., is centre; immediately below it is a broken-down sofa; the door is centre back.

When the curtain rises Fred and Floss are sitting at either side of the table facing each other.

Fred. Thank 'eaven we stopped 'ome to-night.

Floss. And last night.

Fred. And the night before.

Floss. That's right. Comfy, ain't it?

Fred. I reckon we didn't arf ought to feel a bit mingy.

Floss. Oh, we do once in every so often.

Fred. Garn, who does?

FLOSS. I do.

FRED. You do?

FLOSS. Yus, I do.

FRED. Ow! Wot d'you reckon about Alf and Dais? D'you reckon they got together, or d'you think they're moulding about seperate?

FLOSS. 'Ow the 'ell do I know?

FRED. They'll come poppin' in 'ere soon, I shouldn't wonder.

FLOSS. 'Old yer noise, yer making me nervy.

FRED. Orlright, orlright.

FLOSS. 'Ere, I say, are we going to get married again?

FRED. 'Ow d'you feel about it, girl, eh?

FLOSS. Ow, I dunno.

FRED. Well, this week's bin a bit of orlright, we've 'ardly used Solomon Isaacs at all.

FLOSS. Ow, Solomon Isaacs gets me toungue in a knot; wot say we shorten it, eh?

FRED. Wot to?

FLOSS. Sollocks.

FRED. You said it, Sollocks.

FLOSS. You don't 'arf look a treat; wot say I give yer a smacker?

FRED. Garn, Soppy!

(FLOSS *crosses behind table to* FRED—*they kiss.*)

FLOSS. Thanks, Cock.

FRED. Par de too, par de too! Do you 'appen to be booked up for this dance, Lady Hagatha?

FLOSS. Well, I was, but the feller was suddenly took queer.

FRED. 'Ard cheese! Well, let's you and me 'ave a turn and chance it.

(*Gramophone—they dance.*)

Floor's a bit of orlright, eh?

FLOSS. Musn't grumble. 'Ere, ain't that the Grand Duchess Olga over there pickin' 'er nose?

FRED. Ow, yes, 'er old man got corpsed last Toosday comin' 'ome from the gas works.

FLOSS. Wot the 'ell was 'e doin' at the gas works?

FRED. Ow, blowing 'isself out.

(*He turns off gramophone.*)

'Ere, girl, what's your trouble?

FLOSS. Ow, nothin', leave me be. (*Sits on sofa.*)

FRED. Come on, spit it out, spit it out.

FLOSS. I was thinkin' of young Daisy.

FRED. Oh, Dais.

FLOSS. I bet she's properly breaking 'er 'eart.

FRED. Ow, shut yer face; we've 'ad all this out before. We knew the moment we saw one another again it was no use goin' on. (*Joins* FLOSS *on sofa.*)

FLOSS. 'Ere; supposin' we 'adn't 'appened to 'ave met again? Would you 'ave been orlright with Dais?

FRED. I daresay.

FLOSS. Ow, Fred.

FRED. Well, wot of it? You'd 'ave rubbed along orlright with Alf.

FLOSS. Poor old Alf: 'e was gone on me and that's a fact.

FRED. Ain't you lucky?

FLOSS. 'E used to look at me sort of 'opeless and I'd sort of look back; and, oh, I dunno——

FRED. That must 'ave been prime.

FLOSS. 'E used to look after me so lovely—like as if I was something rare and precious.

FRED. Oh, dear, oh dear——

FLOSS. Don't talk so rude.

FRED. Go on, go on; tell us about 'is legs and 'is ears and 'is eyes and 'is lovely curly 'air; go on, tell us.

FLOSS. Mind out yer don't cut yourself, Mr. Sharp.

FRED. That's right; get ratty.

FLOSS. Who's ratty?

FRED. Ow, shut up.

FLOSS. Shut up yourself.

FRED. Well, I'm sick to death of 'earing you keep yappin' about Alf, Alf, Alf, Alf, Alf, Alf——

FLOSS. Sulky great brute!

FRED. 'Ere Floss—Sollocks—Sollocks.

(*Singing interlude.*)

(*Return to sofa.*)

FRED. You don't 'arf get me goin', old girl.

FLOSS. Don't be soft.

FRED. Swing yer dial round a bit, ducks.

FLOSS. 'Ow's that?

FRED. Lubly!

FLOSS. You are a card, and no error.

FRED. We was fair batty, rowin' and muckin' things up the way we did.

FLOSS. That's right.

FRED. D'you remember that row we 'ad at the Elephant?

FLOSS. Not 'arf!

FRED. Goo, weren't we fat 'eads?

FLOSS. Yus, but we ain't no more, are we?

FRED. Yer know, the real trouble that time was Ted Rawlins.

FLOSS. Yer know 'e was nothin' in my young life.

FRED. 'Ow the 'ell was I to know? 'E gave yer presents, didn't 'e?

FLOSS. Presents! A couple of 'bus rides and a bit of white fox.

FRED. Yus, and a mangy-lookin' thing it was, too.

FLOSS. You're a liar; it was a lovely piece and I wear it often.

FRED. Ow, yer do, do you?

FLOSS. Yus, I do, and who's to stop me?

(*Long pause. He goes to table.*)

FRED. Want another Guinness?

FLOSS. I do not.

FRED. Ho, indeed! Well, I do.

FLOSS. Go on, soak, soak, soak, yer sozzling great fool.

FRED. It 'ud take more'n three Guinnesses to sozzle yours truly.

FLOSS. It didn't last Saturday.

FRED. Wot about last Saturday?

FLOSS. Oh, shut up shop, you give me a 'eadache.

FRED (*pouring out another Guinness*). I suppose Ted Rawlins was Temperance?

FLOSS. Well, anyhow, 'e didn't 'iccup on the froth like you do.

FRED. You're funny, you are, ain't yer? Just funny, eh?

(FLOSS *turns on gramophone.*)

FLOSS. Ow, go an' boil yer face.

FRED. Shut up that noise. You're not the only lodger.

FLOSS. Yes, I am. The 'Arris's 'ave gone to the pictures.

FRED. And wot about Mrs. Clark? No ears, I suppose?

FLOSS. Well, if she 'as, she's either awake or dead by this time, yer great fog 'orn!

FRED. Turn off that instrument.

FLOSS. I shall not.

FRED. I will, then——

(*Business—fight over gramophone.*)

FLOSS. You've mucked up the record now.

FRED. And a damned good job, too.

FLOSS. Dirty bully!

FRED. Blimey, Floss—Sollocks, Sollocks!

FLOSS. Sollocks yerself.

(*Etc. etc. etc.—Stand-up fight, ending in undignified struggle on floor.*)

CURTAIN

## TRIO: "BRIGHT YOUNG PEOPLE"

1930

*Verse* 1

Look at us three,
Representative we
Of a Nation renowned for virility,
We've formed a cult of puerility
Just for fun.
You may deplore
The effects of the war
Which are causing the world to decay a bit.
We've found our place and will play a bit
In the sun.
Though Waterloo was won upon the playing fields of
    Eton,
The next war will be photographed, and lost, by Cecil
    Beaton.

*Verse* 2

Things that we do
'Neath the Red, White and Blue,
Though they can't be called happy or glorious,
Certainly keep us notorious.
And it's grand
We've made some chums
In the heart of the slums,

And we ask to our parties the rougher ones.
We find the low class and tougher ones understand,
We know a darling Bolshevik who's taught us Dos Vedanya
And he can sing "God Save the King" and lovely "Rule Britannia."

*Refrain 1*

Bright young people
Ready to do and to dare,
We casually strive
To keep London alive
From Chelsea to Bloomsbury Square.
We fondly imagine we're cynical elves,
In charity tableaux we pose upon shelves.
It's just an excuse to exhibit ourselves.
What could be duller than that?

*Refrain 2*

Bright young people,
Gay to the utmost degree.
We play funny jokes
On more dignified folks
And laugh with extravagant glee.
We give lovely parties that last through the night,
I dress as a woman and scream with delight,
We wake up at lunch time and find we're still tight.
What could be duller than that?

*Refrain 3*

Bright young people,
Don't think our lives are not full.
I make little hats
From Victorian mats
And I work with tin foil and wool.
Our critics are often excessively rude,
To any of my portraits they always allude:
It's me, worked in beads, upside down, in the
nude.
What could be duller than that?

*Refrain 4*

Bright young people,
Making the most of our youth.
They speak in the Press
Of our social success,
But quite the reverse is the truth.
Psychology experts we often perplex,
And doctors have warned us we'll end up as
wrecks.
They take a degree if they find out our sex.
What could be duller than that?

## "ANY LITTLE FISH"

1930

*Verse* 1

I'VE fallen in love with you,
I'm taking it badly,
Freezing, burning,
Tossing, turning,
Never know when to laugh or cry.
Just look what our dumb friends do,
They welcome it gladly.
Passion in a dromedary doesn't go so deep,
Camels when they're mating never sob themselves
to sleep,
Buffaloes can revel in it, so can any sheep.
Why can't I?

*Refrain* 1

Any little fish can swim,
Any little bird can fly,
Any little dog
Or any little cat
Can do a bit of this
And just a bit of that.
Any little horse can neigh
And any little cow can moo,

But I can't do anything at all
But just love you.

*Refrain 2*

Any little cock can crow,
Any little fox can run,
Any little crab
On any little shore
Can have a little dab
And then a little more.
Any little owl can hoot (Towhit towhoo),
And any little dove can coo,
But I can't do anything at all
But just love you.

*Verse 2*

You've pulled me across the brink,
You've chained me and bound me ;
No escape now,
Buy the crêpe now.
When is the funeral going to be ?
Whenever I stop to think,
See Nature all round me,
Then I see how stupidly monogamous I am.
A lion, in the circumstances, wouldn't give a damn,
For if there were no lioness, he'd lie down with a lamb.
Why not me ?

*Refrain 3*

Any little bug can bite,
Any little bee can buzz,

Any little snail
On any little oak
Can feel a little frail
And have a little joke.
Any little frog can jump
Like any little kangaroo,
But I can't do anything at all
But just love you.

*Refrain* 4

Any little duck can quack,
Any little worm can crawl,
Any little mole
Can frolic in the sun
And make a little hole
And have a little fun.
Any little snake can hiss
In any little local Zoo,
But I can't do anything at all
But just love you.

# HALF-CASTE WOMAN

1930

*(The Scene is a cheap café on the water front of any far Eastern port. An electric piano is grinding out some popular tune, and two or three* COUPLES *are dancing. Flashy Tarts, Sailors, Merchantmen, and one or two more or less drunken habitués in creased tropical suits. There is a Chinese woman behind the bar, and a slovenly* WAITER *carrying drinks. He is a half-caste and wears a dirty white coat over black silk trousers.)*

*(When the Curtain rises "* DAISY *" is sitting with her back to the audience with her arms round the necks of two* MERCHANTMEN *in rather grimy white duck uniforms.* DAISY *wears a scarlet or yellow evening dress, very décolletée and covered mostly with sequins. She has several bangles jangling on her arms and lots of false pearls. Her hair is black and sleek, and behind her ear she wears a flower, probably a hibiscus, or a camelia.*

*There is a lot of noise and drunken laughter. Suddenly, outside in the grey dusk three blasts on a ship's syren are heard. The men disentangle themselves from* DAISY, *the* WAITER *brings them the bill, which one of them pays. Four or five people go out into the street. The old* CHINESE WOMAN *rounds the rest of them up until the café is empty except for* DAISY *and the* WAITER. *He staggers off through a bead curtain doorway behind the bar, carrying a tray of glasses. The* OLD WOMAN *shuts the door and locks it. Outside on the water front it is getting lighter, a long way off down the street can be heard the intermittent wailing of some Eastern reed instrument.* DAISY *gets up and goes over to the bar, pours herself out a drink and leans there wearily, her face is grey and tired. Suddenly there comes a rapping at the window. The* OLD WOMAN *looks up and sees one of the* MERCHANTMEN *signing to be let it. She shakes her head.* DAISY *pushes her out of the way and unlocks the door. The* YOUNG MAN *comes in.*)

MAN. I left my hat.

DAISY (*listlessly*). It's there, under the table.

MAN. Thanks. (*He picks it up.*) It's been a swell evening.

DAISY. Has it?

MAN. Haven't you enjoyed it?

DAISY. Like hell I have.

MAN. I've got to get back to the ship now.

DAISY. That's all right with me.

MAN. You were different a little while ago; don't you like me any more?

DAISY. I'm crazy about you, baby; you've just changed everything with your bright trusting blue eyes. Pardon me for yawning.

MAN. Oh, I see. (*He hesitates.*) I'm sorry—— (*He turns to go.*) Good night.

DAISY. Why did you come back?

MAN (*sullenly*). To get my hat.

DAISY. That all?

MAN. Yes. Good night.

DAISY (*suddenly clutching his arm*). Here, here's something to be going on with. (*She kisses him almost fiercely on the mouth.*)

MAN. What did you do that for?

DAISY. Don't you know?

MAN. Daisy—listen—I——

DAISY (*interrupting*). Come back again some day, but don't leave it too long.

(*The ship's syren gives another loud blast.*)

Go on—hurry—— (*She pushes him towards the door.*)

MAN (*taking her into his arms and kissing her tenderly*). Good-bye, old girl.

DAISY (*as he goes*). Give my love to the world.

(*She goes wearily back to the bar.*)

### *"Half-caste Women"*

#### *Verse*

Drink a bit, laugh a bit, love a bit more,
I can supply your need.
Think a bit, chaff a bit. What's it all for?
That's my Eurasian creed.

Sailors with sentimental hearts who love and sail away.
When the Dawn is grey,
Look at me and say

*Refrain*

Half-caste woman,
Living a life apart,
Where did your story begin?
Half-caste woman,
Have you a secret heart
Waiting for someone to win?
Were you born of some queer magic
In your shimmering gown?
Is there something strange and tragic
Deep, deep down?
Half-caste woman,
What are your slanting eyes
Waiting and hoping to see?
Scanning the far horizon
Wondering what the end will be.

*Interlude*

Down along the river
The sky is a-quiver,
For Dawn is beginning to break.
Hear the syrens wailing,
Some big ship is sailing,
And losing my dreams in its wake.
Why should I remember the things that are past,
Moments so swiftly gone?
Why worry, for the Lord knows Time goes on.

Go to bed in daylight,
Try to sleep in vain.
Get up in the evening,
Work begins again.
Tinker tailor, soldier, sailor, rich man, poor
man, beggar man, thief,
Questioning the same refrain.

*Repeat refrain*

## "CITY"

1930

*Verse* I

Only one among millions, Life's a sad routine,
  Striving for a goal that hasn't a meaning.
Lonely, living in shadow, part of a machine.
  Rising from despair the buildings are leaning,
Nearer, nearer each day, pressing Life away.

*Refrain*

    City, why are you casting this spell on me?
  City, what if you crumbled and fell on me?
  Unbelievably tiring, Life passes by me,
    Noise and speed are conspiring to crucify me,
    Ever making me crawl for my daily bread,
    Never letting me rest till my dreams are dead.
    Every weary prisoner some day must be free.
    City, have pity on me!

*Interlude*

Day in, day out,
Life will be soon over and done. Where has it led,
    and why?
Day in, day out,

Where is the moon? Where is the sun? Where is the open sky?
Ever seeking, and believing. Where is hope for us all?
Syrens shrieking, Progress weaving poor Humanity's pall.
Iron, rot; steel, rust,
Speed, noise, death, dust.
Why should we work? Why should we live? Why should we
Even die?

*Repeat refrain*

## "MAD DOGS AND ENGLISHMEN"

1930

*Verse* 1

In tropical climes there are certain times of day
When all the citizens retire
To tear their clothes off and perspire.
It's one of those rules that the greatest fools obey,
Because the sun is much too sultry
And one must avoid its ultry—violet ray.
Papalaka papalaka papalaka boo,
Papalaka papalaka papalaka boo,
Digariga digariga digariga doo,
Digariga digariga digariga doo.
The natives grieve when the white men leave their huts,
Because they're obviously definitely Nuts!

*Refrain* 1

Mad dogs and Englishmen
Go out in the midday sun.
The Japanese don't care to,
The Chinese wouldn't dare to,
Hindoos and Argentines sleep firmly from twelve to
one.
But Englishmen detest a—Siesta.

In the Philippines there are lovely screens
To protect you from the glare.
In the Malay States there are hats like plates
Which the Britishers won't wear.
At twelve noon the native swoon
And no further work is done,
But mad dogs and Englishmen
Go out in the midday sun.

*Verse 2*

It's such a surprise for the Eastern eyes to see,
That tho' the English are effete,
They're quite impervious to heat.
When the white man rides every native hides in glee
Because the simple creatures hope he
Will impale his solar topee—on a tree.
Bolyboly bolyboly bolyboly baa,
Bolyboly bolyboly bolyboly baa,
Habaninny habaninny habaninny haa,
Habaninny habaninny habaninny.
It seems such a shame when the English claim the earth
That they give rise to such hilarity and mirth.

*Refrain 2*

Mad dogs and Englishmen
Go out in the midday sun.
The toughest Burmese bandit
Can never understand it.
In Rangoon the heat of noon
Is just what the natives shun.
They put their Scotch or Rye down—and lie down
In a jungle town where the sun beats down.

To the rage of man and beast
The English garb of the English Sahib
Merely gets a bit more creased.
In Bangkok at twelve o'clock
They foam at the mouth and run,
But mad dogs and Englishmen
Go out in the midday sun.

*Refrain 3*

Mad dogs and Englishmen
Go out in the midday sun.
The smallest Malay rabbit
Deplores this stupid habit.
In Hong Kong they strike a gong
And fire off a noonday gun
To reprimand each inmate—who's in late.
In the mangrove swamps where the python
romps
There is peace from twelve till two.
Even caribous lie around and snooze,
For there's nothing else to do.
In Bengal, to move at all
Is seldom, if ever done,
But mad dogs and Englishmen
Go out in the midday sun.